I0139059

Common Grace

And The Call Of The Gospel

Common Grace
and the Call of the Gospel

George M. Ella

Go *publications*

Go Publications
Gibb Hill Farm, Ponsonby, Cumbria, CA20 1BX, ENGLAND

British Library Cataloguing in Publication Data available

ISBN 978-1-908475-09-1

Printed and bound in Great Britain
by Lightning Source UK Ltd.

Table of Contents

Introduction

The doctrine of common grace is the idea that God has a grace, or goodness, which is universally bestowed on all men. Supporters of the doctrine use it to explain everything from indiscriminate rainfall and sunshine on both the good and the wicked to a universal desire in God to save all men, even those who will ultimately go to hell.

Dr Ella's book is a timely and useful look at this teaching. His brief but probing examination concentrates on an effort by some recent writers to construct a basis for the so-called 'free offer of the gospel' in common grace teaching. He questions the notion that common grace is a route to saving faith through the preaching of a gospel ultimately grounded in natural theology. He concludes that the 'common grace' gospel is based on unscriptural views of nature, man, God and salvation.

The author shows that the gospel call does not derive from a universal but frustrated desire in God to save all men, nor from a grace that is common to all. Rather the gospel brings grace to the elect by the direct, distinguishing power of the Holy Spirit according to God's eternal purpose for the salvation of His people. The common grace teaching that Christ died theoretically for all sinners but effectively for only some is thus to be rejected as a false gospel.

Peter L. Meney

Part 1: The Gospel Of Common Grace

An innovating concept of salvation

The topic of common grace was dealt with briefly in my booklet *The Free Offer and the Call of the Gospel*, but since writing on that subject, there has been a flood of publications from the pens of professed Reformed authors using common grace as a justification for their free-offer doctrine. On the whole, these works have explored new grounds for evangelism, suggesting innovating concepts of salvation. Many, such as *The Free Offer of the Gospel*, by John Murray and Ned Stonehouse, originally written in 1948,[1] and republished in 2001 under Murray's name only, have sadly been too shallow, controversial, and speculative to serve as a solid basis for Christian evangelism. Also, following Murray's lead, other recent works are based on pseudo-academic, critical renderings of the Bible text to accommodate new theories concerning the contents and scope of the gospel. These self-styled Reformed authors claim that in order to preach

[1] This version was commented on in my book on the free offer.

successfully today, we must abandon all traditional Christian ideas of Scripture, God, man and the gospel. They tell us that successful preachers of the past such as Crisp, Davis, Romaine, Toplady, Hervey, Traill, Gill and Hawker were wrong in basing their gospel on the commands of God and the vicarious, penal sacrifice of Christ for His people. The modern, successful way, they say, is to base evangelism on what they call common grace or natural law which, they tell us, reveals God's saving grace to all so that Christ can be called 'Everybody's Saviour'[2]. Obviously, if they can prove their point that Christ is everybody's Saviour, then we owe a great debt to these preachers of a new way to God and we must recognise that the churches have been in darkness since the dawn of Christianity.

The origin of the common grace gospel

There is no common definition of common grace. Its heyday was in Roman Catholic Scholasticism when the theological emphasis moved from sin and grace to the natural and the supernatural. Salvation was seen as a steady climb from the one to the other. Common grace led to saving grace, to the beatific vision. This idea of progression was modified by a number of Reformed divines, particularly Dutch, to describe the external working of the Holy Spirit in nature and on man but not the inner working of saving grace. Thus the external work of the Spirit was variously seen as 1. Natural Common Grace on all creation; 2. Universal Common Grace on all life; 3. General Common Grace on human beings; 4. Covenant Common

---

[2] So Malcolm Watts in his *Free Offer of the Gospel.*

Grace on all those under the Covenant whether elect or not. Some divines have accepted all four interpretations. Arminians have kept the idea that by contemplating common grace the mind can find enough reasons to accept Christ as Saviour. Others argue that an awareness of what God has done in nature lays upon man the duty of believing in Him savingly. Both these errors have been combined in Fullerism which brings us back to Scholasticism which sees common grace as a step in the *ordo salutis* (order of salvation), linking the natural with the supernatural. This Scholasticism is now rampant in Reformed circles.

Creating an enemy alien picture

A new organization establishes itself all the quicker if it can produce a long acquainted negative opposite from which it can distance itself. Thus the Nazis developed their stereotyped *Feindbild*,[3] allegedly demonstrating the superiority of the Japhetic over the Semitic. The idea thus propagated by modern common grace enthusiasts is that their 'positive side' is the original rather than the 'negative side' which grew up in opposition to it. A major strategy of these common-grace gospellers is thus to 'create', or rather 'invent' a 'negative side' or 'enemy picture' against which they can propagate their 'positive' propaganda. Common-gracers, of course, pick on those representatives of Orthodoxy who are as far away from their new general gospel of common grace as could be for their enemy picture. They thus blacken the reputation of full-gospel preachers of yester-year who were widely followed, and brand

---

[3] Enemy picture.

them all as 'Hyper-Calvinists' or 'Antinomians' and those who were always against the 'positive' truth. Having convinced themselves that they have swept out the dirty stables, they feel they can then legitimately and conveniently bring in their new, dried tares, chaff and stubble which they present as the real clean, positive gospel. The 'enemy' thus created is certainly at enmity with the wishy-washy gospel of the common-gracers who create a bogus fabrication of the cause of God and truth, which, they maintain, is the proper 'free offer' of salvation to be given to all.

Deniers of common grace claimed to be Hyper-Calvinists

In his highly controversial essay *A Primer on Hyper-Calvinism*, Phillip R. Johnson sees common grace as a major criterion in spotting heretics. If a person, says Johnson, 'denies that there is such a thing as common grace', he is a 'Hyper-Calvinist'. Johnson defines a Hyper-Calvinist as one who 'emphasises divine sovereignty to the exclusion of human responsibility'. Incidentally, none of those whom Johnson brands as Hypers come under that category, and it is no difficult task to prove that such as Ryland, Gill and Huntington, i.e. Johnson's 'Hypers', had an infinitely higher view of man's responsibility for his state than Johnson and his fellow common-grace gospellers. However, an effigy must be set up and burnt and common-gracers mark their effigy to be destroyed with the features of those who preach up God's sovereign mercies and preach down man's capabilities. Indeed, they confuse man's responsibilities with man's capabilities and argue that as man is responsible for his sin, he must have the natural ability to do something about it.

Attempts to define common grace

After thus affirming what he cannot, or at least does not, prove, Johnson goes on to say:

> The idea of common grace is implicit throughout Scripture. 'The Lord is good to all: and his tender mercies are over all his works' (Psalm 149). 'He doth execute the judgment of the fatherless and widow, and loveth the stranger, in giving food and raiment. Love ye therefore the stranger: for ye were strangers in the land of Egypt' (Deuteronomy 10:18-19). Love your enemies, bless them that hate you, and pray for them which despitefully use you, and persecute you; that ye may be the children of your Father which is in heaven' (Matthew 5:44-45).
>
> The distinction between common grace and special grace closely parallels the distinction between the general call and the effective call. Common grace is extended to everyone. It is God's goodness to humanity in general whereby God graciously restrains the full expression of sin and mitigates sin's destructive effects in human society.
>
> Common grace imposes moral restraints on people's behaviour, maintains a semblance of order in human affairs, enforces a sense of right and wrong through conscience and civil government, enables men and women to appreciate beauty and goodness, and imparts blessings of all kinds to elect and non-elect alike. God causes His sun to rise on the evil and the good, and

> sends rain on the righteous and the unrighteous (Matthew 5:45). That is common grace.[4]

Common grace and 'everybody's Saviour'

Common grace, is thus for Johnson, not merely the providential fact that God allows the sun to shine on the just and the unjust but is akin to a general call to salvation which God gives to every one. He goes on to argue that this common grace is the means by which God displays His compassionate love to all men. This compassionate love is, in turn, the reason why God offers saving grace to all men everywhere. Yet, after arguing enthusiastically that God's compassionate love for all sinners gives us our basis for freely offering Christ to all men, Johnson takes it all back and tells us that though God exercises *compassionate love* in this way, He yet withholds his *redemptive love* from the non-elect. Thus Johnson presents not only common grace as an immoral farce but also his free offer of the gospel. Johnson's weird message is that God loves those sinners compassionately whom He sends to hell. What a horrid gospel to be offered to all men!

Though Malcolm Watts, in his The *Free Offer of the Gospel*[5] comes very near to this position, he states that he is not 'totally satisfied' with the link-up between common grace and the call to salvation. Nevertheless, he believes that there is a common denominator amongst all men which makes

---

4 *A Primer on Hyper-Calvinism*, Phillip R. Johnson, Sword and Trowel, March, 2001, p. 14

5 *Emmanuel Church Magazine*, Salisbury, Vol. 13, No 7, p. 6; No 8, pp. 3-4, 2001-2002.

Christ 'everybody's Saviour and this is why it is lawful for all to apply to Him for salvation'. What Watts means by 'lawful', he does not explain. However, the idea of a common law is always very near those definitions of common grace which are put forward as a basis for salvation. William Huntington is, for instance, called the 'godfather' of Hyper-Calvinism by Johnson because he 'denied that the moral law is binding as a rule of life on the Christian.' Actually, this is quite untrue. Huntington believed that his people loved the moral law, using it lawfully, (i.e. for its God-given purpose) far more than those Antinomians i.e. some followers of Andrew Fuller and some of the Countess of Huntingdon's men, who misused it. These placed all sinners under grace but all the saints under the Mosaic Law. This was a reversal of the doctrine of salvation, he argued. To denounce a man as a Hyper for such a balanced display of orthodoxy is, to say the least, grossly unfair. Johnson recommends John Ryland Jun. as being on 'his side', but Ryland, in his biography of Fuller, vindicates Gill and Brine, whom modern common-gracers lump with Huntington, from the charge of Antinomianism. Ryland Junior also comes very near to Huntington's anti-Antinomian position when he accuses 'some Calvinistic Methodists' and 'especially those in Lady Huntingdon's Connexion' of such 'false Calvinism'; that false Calvinism being Antinomianism.[6]

Common grace and duty-faith

Andrew Fuller's view of the gospel was that it was embedded in the moral law. The law was there to show man the way to God

---

[6] *Memoirs of Mr. Fuller*, pp. 6, 7.

and the gospel is there to encourage man to keep the law. It is thus no surprise to see him linking law closely with faith. In his brief article entitled *Faith Required by the Moral Law*, Fuller argues:

> I have no doubt but that a belief of the gospel of Christ, even such a one as is connected with salvation, is required by the moral law, and is one of its most weighty matters; for the moral law requires love to God with all the heart; and love to God would certainly lead us to embrace any revelation which he should make of himself; such a revelation especially in which the glory of God is provided for in the highest degree. But the term faith, in Matt. xxii. 23, I consider as synonymous with fidelity or veracity, being ranked with judgment and mercy, which are duties of the second table.[7]

The supposed fact that the first law tablet spoke of what attitude we should have towards God and the second to what duties evolve from this attitude, is the basis of the common-gracers doctrine of Old Testament duty faith. Admittedly, they claim that this Old Testament teaching points to a greater fulfiller of the law, but they also teach that through keeping the old law and its duties, we should automatically be able to keep the new gospel and its duties. Man, here, thus rivals Christ. This does not disturb the common-gracers as they see salvation as teamwork between God and man. But Christ in fulfilling the law, did not just fulfil the first tablet, revealing

---

[7] *Works*, Vol. III, p. 781.

Himself to the sinner, but He also fulfilled the second tablet, taking over the law duties. As every man has broken these laws, no man can claim that they are applicable to him as if he had never broken them. Man can no longer use either tablet in order to get right with God. Common-gracers always soft-pedal on the first tablet but always emphasise that the Christian is still under the second tablet. As Christ has fulfilled both tablets, no man can claim that either the first or the second tablet concerning duties is still there for him to pursue. The common-grace teaching of a common duty of mankind to believe in Christ savingly is thus merely part and parcel of the condemning but not saving function of the law which they misunderstand. Mankind cannot believe savingly through law-duties but can be saved through the perfect obedience and saving grace of the only One who can and has fulfilled those duties. Faith is thus not a law duty but a gospel grace. It has nothing to do with a fictitious and general common grace but all to do with a specific and discriminating saving grace.

John Murray on common grace

In the current 30 paged reprint, of Murray's *The Free Offer of the Gospel*, the author argues along common-grace lines which he purports to find in Matthew 5:44-48. What he gives us, however, are philosophical views of bye-gone years concerning natural law, Grotianism and Latitudinarianism. The gist of what he says, with my comments is:

1. God's Providence in nature is revealed to all, that is, all mankind is under God's loving-kindness. Here, Murray is apparently forgetting that sin marred all, including nature, and that nature is often, as the poet says 'red in tooth and claw'.

However, a main doctrine of the common-grace enthusiasts is that the fall refers to moral and not natural characteristics, so they obviously see nature as if she were pre-fallen.

2. In God 'there is a will to the realization of what he has not decretively willed, a pleasure toward that which he has not been pleased to decree.' What this means is perhaps anyone's guess, but Murray appears to be saying that something stops God from doing what He wills to do and prevents Him doing what He is pleased to do.

3. Christ 'willed the bestowal of his saving and protecting grace upon those whom neither the Father nor he decreed thus to save and protect.' Thus we have a 'godhead' who not only cannot stick to his own will but who has obviously several different wills, the one contradicting the other. In other words, this god is arbitrary, though impotent, in the enacting of his wills.

4. 'The will of God for repentance and salvation is universal and in this God shows his loving-kindness to those whom he has not decreed to save.' This is the common-gracers' pragmatic idea that the Atonement is sufficient for all but only applicable to those who accept it. This is blatant Arminianism but Fullerites call it 'Strict Calvinism'. It is all a matter of definition!

5. We can thus conclude, says Murray, that his inferences on Matthew 5:44-48, are correct, namely that 'the full and free offer of the gospel is a grace bestowed upon all.' Of this grace, he says, 'The grace offered is nothing less than salvation in its richness and fullness.' This goes beyond anything I have met up with amongst the Arminians and cannot be distinguished from Universalism. Any reader of intelligence will automatically understand here that Murray is

equating 'bestow' with 'offer' and saying that what is offered to all is bestowed on all.[8]

This, Babel-like belief, our common-gracers tell us, must be accepted or one is not a Bible believing Christian but a Hyper-Calvinist. What makes this alleged 'good news' all the worse is that Murray tells us that the text of Matthew 5:44-48 on which he builds his common-grace theory, is corrupt and our only means of rightly understanding God's Word is to follow Murray's radical repairs. After reading several pages of Murray's 'criticism with a penknife', paring his gospel to shape, I turned to Johnson's similarly daring account in his *Primer on Hyper-Calvinism*, only to read that if we 'Hypers' do not follow his quite unorthodox teaching, we 'twist the gospel message'.[9] Apparently these men feel that we must twist Scripture otherwise 'we twist the gospel message'.

Common grace makes all men equal before God

The theory behind this ancient but newly revised approach is that common grace addresses all men equally before God and is thus a fitting basis on which to offer salvation to all. One of the most vocal contenders for this new gospel of confusion which tells us that God both wills and does not will to save all, is Erroll Hulse who claims he walks in John Murray's, Abraham Kuyper's and even John Calvin's footsteps. Hulse's views give us the clearest proof that following the two wills theory of God leads to two totally different and contradictory gospels. Hulse feels he can take both in his stride, oblivious to

---

8 Summarised with actual words in quotes.

9 *Op. cit.*, p. 12.

the Carmel call concerning halting between two opinions and the New Testament call that two cannot walk together if they do not agree[10]. But Hulse delights, he tells us, in believing the paradoxical and he finds his view of Christianity such a paradox.

In order to understand Hulse's new gospel as described in his booklet *The Free Offer*, we must examine his view of common grace and what it entails. Hulse begins his section on *The Doctrine of Common Grace* in his booklet by asking if there is a grace common to all; a grace that even the non-elect can enjoy. Hulse, answers his question in the affirmative, pointing out that God showed His grace to all by promising never to destroy the world by flood again. Then, quoting Acts 14:17 and Acts 17:24, Hulse argues how God gives natural life to all so that all should seek the Lord because they perhaps might find Him. He then turns to Paul's words at the beginning of Romans relating that the whole creation testifies to God's character and glory. He concludes, following Murray and Stonehouse, that God allows the sun to shine on the just and the unjust. So far, so good.

Leaping from common to saving grace

Having established such a common grace, Hulse comes to his second heading *The connection between Common Grace and the Free Offer of the Gospel*. Hitherto, he has given convincing proof for a *Providence* common to all. I would prefer the old, well-tried term, Providence, myself, as its meaning is relatively clear but our common-gracers do not seem to be able to

[10] 1 Kings 18:21; Amos 3:3; 2 Corinthians 6:14

distinguish between what they call *common* and what they call *saving* grace. The sun does shine on the just and the unjust and, according to Scripture, though fallen man does not see this, the whole creation testifies to God's glory. So here, we see a complication coming into Hulse's theory. Though there is a grace or Providence common to all, this is not perceived by all. The long chain of Scriptural references which Hulse gives to demonstrate common grace, also shows that those who remain in their sin are dead to such displays of God's love. Indeed, Paul tells sinful man that he is not aware of God's grace at all, whether common or saving, and that nature speaks to the unsaved sinner in vain, leaving man without any claim on or right to God's grace whatsoever! Mankind is not only naturally blind to God's saving grace, he is naturally blind to Providence.

Now, Hulse takes a great exegetical hop, skip and jump. Based on what he has said, but drawing contrary conclusions to the old orthodox Pauline approach concerning the purpose of natural theology, he asks, 'But does God wish the very highest good for men, the highest blessing being eternal salvation?' Here, an honest reply would be, 'You have not given us evidence enough to answer. You merely speak about common grace which only Christians can recognize and not about saving grace which enables Christians to recognize grace in whatever form. You have given no proof that common grace turns common man to a common salvation.' Surprisingly, however, Hulse answers his own hypothetical question in the affirmative, believing he has demonstrated that common grace incorporates saving grace.

The search for a saving factor in common grace

Next, Hulse re-examines his common grace passages to show that common grace is really saving grace. By now, however, Hulse's readers will probably be asking at least three questions:

Firstly, if man is unable by his fallen nature to understand common grace, if there is such a phenomenon, how will he be able to apply Hulse's theory to his own predicament savingly?

Secondly, what is instrumental to salvation in these common grace passages?

Thirdly, how does the fact that it rains on the just and unjust make unjust men just besides merely wet?

Hulse has no answers to these questions, or rather he does not seem to envisage such displays of doubt. Such paradoxes are items of faith, he argues. Indeed the long unexplained list of references Hulse gives us allegedly on common grace, on examination, show that God either rebukes man for failing to see common grace or that His saving grace is quite a different matter to common grace.

Even when Hulse lists Isaiah 1:16-20 (the blessings of salvation and terrors of rejection); Matthew 11:28-30 (Come unto me all that labour and are heavy laden) and Revelation 3:20 (Behold I stand at the door and knock), without exegesis, he still believes he is talking about common grace and sums up by saying:

> Common grace, then, finds its highest expression in that desire and will of God not only for fallen man's temporal well-being but for his soul's salvation and eternal happiness.

Leaving out the missing-link

It would appear here that Hulse is actually saying that common grace is really and truly saving grace and salvation is God's desire and will for all men. However, Hulse has not even begun to prove that his common grace theory includes God's saving will for all sinners. He has left out his missing link. What he has done is listed texts which he alleges show that all earth-dwellers enjoy the same earth to a like extent and then listed texts which show that all believers will enjoy heaven to a like extent and then claims both kinds of texts reveal God's saving will to all and are talking ultimately about the same thing. Taking the term 'will' at its normal semantic face value, we cannot imagine God willing all men's salvation without being successful in accomplishing it. Not wanting to misunderstand Hulse, I turned to his mentor, John Murray, for clarification. Here, there was no mistaking Murray's claim. He writes, referring to the common grace bestowed on all:

> Such grace is necessarily a manifestation of love or lovingkindness in the heart of God. And this lovingkindness is revealed to be of a character or kind that is correspondent with the grace bestowed. The grace offered is nothing less than salvation in its richness and fullness. The love or lovingkindness that lies back of that offer, is not anything less: it is the will to that salvation.[11]

---

[11] *The Free Offer of the Gospel*, Banner of Truth, p. 30.

Common grace saves no one

Hulse leaves his readers with the antinomy (Hulse's euphemism for the inner contradictions of his theory) that though sovereign God wills to save all in common grace, including Cain, man's agency (again Hulse's term), prevents Him. The Scriptures, however, declare that saving grace knows no such scepticism. Paul in Galatians 1:4, speaking to the church, says Christ 'gave himself for our sins, that he might deliver us from this present evil world, according to the *will* of God and our Father.' Such a passage leaves common grace men cold because, in keeping with Murray, they argue that Christ has a different will to His Father's. For the Triune Unity, they have substituted a disunity similar to that found in Greek polytheism. However, not for nothing does Paul go on to say, 'I marvel that ye are so soon removed from him that called you into the grace of Christ unto another gospel: which is not another; but there be some that trouble you, and would pervert the gospel of Christ.' This passage clearly informs us that the gospel of salvation in Christ is not a common grace gospel but one radically different. To reject this difference is to preach a sham gospel. Hebrews 10 clearly states that Christ came to do the *will* of the Father and by that same *will* those given Him by the Father are sanctified and by that same *will* all those for whom Christ died are by one atoning offering perfected for ever. This is proof enough that any doctrine of evangelism must make the sure and certain work of Jesus Christ on the cross and its consequences the grounds of our salvation and thus the basis for all preaching – and not wild tales of wind and weather.

Gospel secrets not to be divulged

One of the main reasons why common-grace gospellers have a low view of preachers of the whole gospel to the whole man is that they claim that such preachers pretend to give away secrets. They thus condemn great Christians of the past such as Tobias Crisp, John Ryland Senior, William Romaine, William Huntington, John Gill, Augustus Toplady and Robert Hawker who would not dilute their gospel to suit what their critics call 'human agency'. These men preached Christ's victorious crucifixion accomplishments, the eternal union of Christ with His Bride; Christ's faith and righteousness imputed to His people, election, predestination and the justifying, saving decrees of God in and from eternity and a faith which endures. They preached repentance and faith wherever they went, realizing that such deep things of God are to be found alone in God's saving grace and not in the natural character of man. One cannot possibly preach repentance and faith on a common grace basis.

Common-grace gospellers call such preachers of righteousness 'Hyper-Calvinists' and 'Antinomians', claiming, against plain historical facts, that holders of such full-gospel doctrines refused to evangelise and only preached to the already saved, pretending to disclose to them secrets which God had not revealed. The 'proof' they give for this astonishing accusation is that the common-grace call of the gospel does not include such comforting doctrines as election, union with Christ and the eternal preservation of God's loved ones. These are God's 'secrets', they tell us, which we, too, must keep secret. Thus, he who preaches such gospel gems, which Christians hitherto thought were clearly revealed in Scripture, is preaching 'another gospel' to theirs. The question is, which gospel saves us; the gospel of natural religion or the gospel of saving grace? These are two radically different gospels, not the same one as common-gracers would have us believe.

Preaching not what God does but what He desires

Here the common grace gospellers tell us that they are misunderstood. It is not that they deny the gospel of saving grace, they argue in their defence, it is that we must not preach *what God actually does* in salvation but *what God desires to do* and God desires to save all men. The great snag with this pseudo-gospel, however, is that it is a gospel of deceit. Such as Murray, Johnson and Hulse know very well that God does not save all, so why do they pretend He does in their preaching? They answer provokingly, 'To show that God is actually well-meaning to sinners and has a will to save all.' Our only sober reply to this must be, 'Who are they trying to fool?' They are certainly neither doing man nor God any service in preaching such a false gospel. Telling sinners who are dead in trespasses and sins that God has a salvation prepared for each and every one of them and following Fuller and Finney in telling everyone that God loves them, so they should love Him back, might please man but it will not save him.

Part 2: The Gospel Of Deceit Analysed

Claiming Calvin's backing

Hulse, Watts, Johnson and John Murray, as Fuller before them, all claim that they are building on Calvin's teaching. Indeed, they claim they are the only true Calvinists. It is true that Calvin speaks against speculating about God's secrets and rightly asks, 'Who knows the mind of God?' However, he makes it very clear that the very gospel of salvation, which modern common-gracers erroneously call God's secrets, has been manifested to our age and outlined throughout the Scriptures. Fullerites claim that this full-gospel is either only for believers or not suitable for preaching at all. It is a religious taboo for them to say that Jesus died for the elect but not for every man. In this, they follow Fuller, often far too closely for their own conscience's comfort. Their mentor, obviously contending *against* Calvin, said:

> There was no necessity for the apostles to publish the Divine purpose to mankind in their addresses to them. These were not designed as a rule of action, either for

> the preachers or the hearers. It was sufficient for them both that Christ was ready to pardon and accept of any sinner whatever that should come unto him. It was equally sufficient, on the other hand, if, after people believed, they were taught these truths which relate to the purposes of grace on their behalf, with a view to cut off all the glorying in themselves, and that they might learn to ascribe the whole *difference* between themselves and others to the mere sovereign grace of God. Hence it is that the chief of those scriptures which we conceive to hold forth a limitation of design in the death of Christ, or any other doctrine of *discriminating* grace, are such as were addressed to believers.[12]

This reductionalist attitude which teaches that the full gospel is not to be preached to unsaved sinners but to believers only is the plague of modern evangelism. Nowadays, and here modern Hyper-Fullerites like Hulse are far more restricted than Fuller ever was, most evangelism which has developed from Fullerism and the New Divinity teaching never gets beyond the initial 'general call', so frightened are those preachers of displaying the sovereignty of God in His works. They prefer to keep such essential parts of the gospel 'secret' even from believers.

Happily, the very people whom common-gracers denounce for not preaching the full (i.e. their) gospel, freely preach all God's revealed truths which Fullerites keep in the dark, these being particularly the doctrines of grace. Furthermore, Calvin's works

---

[12] *Works*, Reply to Philanthropos, Vol. II, p. 495.

clearly show that he has obviously little in common with these preachers of common grace. In Vol. II, Book III, Chapter XXI of his *Institutes* dealing with election and predestination, Calvin affirms:

> There are others who, when they would cure this disease, recommend that the subject of predestination should scarcely if ever be mentioned, and tell us to shun every question concerning it as we would a rock. Although their moderation is justly commendable in thinking that such mysteries should be treated with moderation, yet because they keep too far within the proper measure, they have little influence over the human mind, which does not readily allow itself to be curbed. Therefore, in order to keep the legitimate course in this matter, we must return to the word of God, in which we are furnished with the right rule of understanding. For Scripture is the school of the Holy Spirit, in which as nothing useful and necessary to be known has been omitted, so nothing is taught but what it is of importance to know. Every thing, therefore delivered in Scripture on the subject of predestination, we must beware of keeping from the faithful, lest we seem either maliciously to deprive them of the blessing of God, or to accuse and scoff at the Spirit, as having divulged what ought on any account to be suppressed ...
>
> I admit that profane men lay hold of the subject of predestination to carp, or cavil, or snarl, or scoff. But if their petulance frightens us, it will be necessary to conceal all the principal articles of faith, because they

and their fellows leave scarcely one of them unassailed with blasphemy. A rebellious spirit will display itself no less insolently when it hears that there are three persons in the divine essence, than when it hears that God when he created man foresaw every thing that was to happen to him. Nor will they abstain from their jeers when told that little more than five thousand years have elapsed since the creation of the world. For they will ask, Why did the power of God slumber so long in idleness? In short, nothing can be stated that they will not assail with derision. To quell their blasphemies, must we say nothing concerning the divinity of the Son and Spirit? Must the creation of the world be passed over in silence? No! The truth of God is too powerful, both here and everywhere, to dread the slanders of the ungodly, ...

Those, however, who are so cautious and timid, that they would bury all mention of predestination in order that it may not trouble weak minds, with what colour, pray, will they cloak their arrogance, when they indirectly charge God with a want of due consideration, in not having foreseen a danger for which they imagine that they prudently provide? Whoever, therefore, throws obloquy on the doctrine of predestination, openly brings a charge against God, as having inconsiderately allowed something to escape from him which is injurious to the Church.

The predestination by which God adopts some to the hope of life, and adjudges others to eternal death, no man who would be thought pious ventures simply to deny; but it is greatly cavilled at, especially by those who make prescience its cause. By predestination we mean the eternal decree of God, by which he determined with himself whatever he wished to happen with regard to every man. All are not created on equal terms, but some are preordained to eternal life, others to eternal damnation; and, accordingly, as each has been created for one or other of these ends, we say that he has been predestinated to life or to death.

Calvin can thus sum up:

The doctrine of predestination is to be preached, not passed over in silence.

Fuller on man's agency in salvation

Andrew Fuller is a total puzzle on salvation. He often speaks like a convinced believer in the doctrines of grace but on other occasions he re-defines his terms giving them new contents and outdoes even Finney in his bringing down the gospel to what he feels are its basic elements. At times his over-simplifications do not meet the gospel facts at all as when he sums up the gospel, claiming that God 'requires them (fallen creatures) to love him with all their hearts, the same as if they had never apostatized'![13] This is, indeed, how Fuller often describes man's agency in salvation. The sinner must believe as if he had never sinned, Fuller tells us, but not with a view to gaining lost favour but simply because it is a divine precept, a

[13] *The Gospel Worthy of all Acceptation*, Vol. II, pp. 375, 376.

law, and the gospel 'graciously adds the promise of salvation' to that law. Here, again, we have the old New Divinity teaching on the probationary state of the sinner before God. Here, also, we have a strange view of belief indeed. A belief which has not even accepted that which makes belief belief! This, however, is Fuller's view of the whole process of justification. Even when God's Word says that God justifies the ungodly, Fuller argues that we cannot take this literally because Paul is talking about those who already have a degree of godliness. They are thus ungodly godly. It is not that a sinner is ungodly until he becomes a Christian, it is that he is ungodly as a Christian, too. We are thus to understand that Romans 4:5 is actually speaking about justified Christians and not sinners who become justified. To 'prove' this, Fuller argues that there is no justification without repentance, so as repentance comes before justification and repentance is a godly thing, it cannot be said that a person is ungodly immediately before justification. It escapes Fuller here that repentance in time is granted to those whom God has justified from eternity.[14] Indeed, here is another piece of word conjuring on the part of Fullerites. They will not accept the 18th century vocabulary speaking of the Spirit making sinners *sensible* to the gospel but Fuller went much further than this and spoke of a *holy disposition* fallen creatures must have before justification. They must have a godly state of mind in order to be justified. But Fullerites see no confusion here as they teach that belief comes under man's law-bound agency and the promising of salvation is God's

---

[14] See Fuller's essays on Justification in Vol. III of his *Works*, particularly his *Remarks on Justifying the Ungodly*.

provision which meets man's belief. It is as if God says to man, 'You do your bit and I will do mine.' However, the old maxim, 'God helps those who help themselves' hardly applies to salvation. In all Fullerite theories of salvation, they very rarely describe God as active but He is invariably the passive partner, waiting for man to initiate and activate his own salvation. If man does not use this initiative, he is lost.

The appeal of the common-grace gospel

Hulse's gospel appeal, and his reasoning with sinners that logically follows from it, is exemplified in the following words:

> This world in which we walk is like a sea, storms arise; we are ready to perish; while we do not cry to Christ for help, is it his fault if we be drowned? If the doctor comes to your door with an excellent remedy and ready to heal you, but you are against his admittance are you not deserving to die?[15]

This is not the gospel call of saving grace at all. We preach a salvation for those who cannot and will not cry out for help when sinking or cannot and will not open doors to doctors when ill. We see their plight and illness in that they are entirely incapable of any such action in salvation. We preach a gospel of God taking the active initiative, pulling men out of their plight when they never even suspect that they are in dire trouble. When a person is too ill to react to a knock at the door, no human doctor worth his salt would turn round and leave his

[15] *The Free Offer*, p. 9.

patient. Those men who carried their friend to the Saviour for healing, did not stop at a blocked doorway but uncovered the roof so as to lay the sick man before Jesus' feet. When God chooses to save and heal us, no stormy sea or well-shut door can prevent Him from carrying out His saving work. His work is one of grace and grace means that it is entirely of God and not man. Grace, to be grace, cannot be teamwork between man and God but must come undeservedly, even unexpectedly and it often comes suddenly without one knowing about it till it comes. Grace is pure mercy and never awaits human agency before God dispenses it. Even the first cry to God for help, is a work of grace on God's part.

Not a giving but a taking

When criticizing the Marrow Men and James Hervey, commonly known as *The Preacher of Righteousness*, for their teaching on salvation as a gift, which he appears not to have understood, Fuller tells us, 'The gospel is a feast freely provided, and sinners of mankind are freely invited to partake of it. There is no mention of any gift, or grant, distinct from this, but this itself is ground sufficient.'[16] Of course, in another context, coupled with teaching that saving grace is a gift of God, such a passage would be encouraging to the one moved by the Spirit but Fuller writes these words to emphasise that faith is not a gift but a duty and God gives this faith to those who perform their duty. Faith is only then a gift when man stretches out and gives it to himself. Thus God merely provides salvation, waiting for man to take it and apply it. Fallen creatures are to behave in the

---

[16] *Works*, Vol. II, p. 338.

gospel as if they were not fallen and give themselves that saving grace which they are free to take from the Father's deposit of grace.[17] Here we have the doubly deceitful gospel of common-grace: they tell sinners that they should behave as if they had never sinned and then preach that God wills to save those whom He will not save. Johnson tells us that the weakness of Hyper-Calvinism is that it 'encourages introspection in the search to know whether or not one is elect' and thus 'assurance tends to be elusive'.[18] One can imagine those falling under this mock-gospel not only being totally confused about both election and assurance but rejecting the lot as the silliest humbug they have ever heard!

Saving grace is all of grace

True preachers of saving grace teach that God leads those who cannot grasp out and feed themselves to the table and He nurtures them Himself, starting with baby milk and then going on to strong meat. One does not expect a helpless one to initiate his own salvation. Common-gracers do because they do not look upon man as helpless and thus leave the Fall out of their preaching programme. Relying on man's natural capacities, Fuller repeatedly claimed that there were no impossibilities in man for gaining duty-faith salvation. Common grace enthusiasts see their probationers' personal rejection of Christ as that breach in the rules of their probation which condemns them. They could have accepted Christ, but they refused. Biblical salvation shows that no one can accept

[17] Ibid, p. 335-336. Part I and II should be consulted for Fuller's full argument.

[18] *A Primer on Hyper-Calvinism*, p. 10.

Christ on Fullerite grounds because no one is on probation. All are already condemned after Adam's breach of his probation. None can trust in Christ but, nevertheless, Christ redeems His elect amongst the condemned ones.

Heads running away with hearts

Phillip R. Johnson, in his *Primer on Hyper-Calvinism*, castigates John Ryland Senior severely for not following common-grace-natural-law devotees, though Ryland evangelised the country highways and bye-ways of areas laid waste by Hulse's, Watts' and Murray's Latitudinarian forerunners. Ryland increased his Nottingham church seven-fold, doing also great evangelistic work in city areas. However, when his son took over the work, it dwindled and Ryland Junior ostracized those who had been close to his father. So too, Peter Toon, in his articles on Hyper-Calvinism, on whom Johnson obviously relies,[19] criticizes one after the other great men of God and evangelists who led hundreds and thousands to Christ. Toon denies that this was a work of the gospel as, according to his misguided view of things, these men had no gospel for sinners. Hulse, when faced with the undeniable fact that Gadsby led hundreds and more to Christ though a 'Hyper', the common-grace enthusiast does not modify his view of Hyperism, nor does he conclude that William Gadsby could never have been a Hyper, but merely tells us that Gadsby's heart ran away with his head. Perhaps here, Hulse's head is running away with his heart.

---

[19] See Toon's entry on Hyper-Calvinism in the *New Dictionary of Theology* and his book of that name.

The Second Downgrade Controversy

It is well-known in world Christendom of the brave stance of Charles Haddon Spurgeon against the downgrading going on in his denomination and Christianity at large during the 1880s. This led to his withdrawal from the Baptist Union which had become a creedless, para-church organization with a membership bound only by the common ritual of water immersion. At the start of the controversy, it appeared that it was a case of Spurgeon against the rest of the world, but gradually it became clear to thousands of believers that it was false charity to worship with those who were denying the vicarious work of Christ, justification by His righteousness and the unity of the Trinity and campaigning for a natural religion under the guise of evangelical Christianity.[20] So as not to give his readers the feeling that this was merely Spurgeon's own private feud, the *Sword and the Trowel* gave ample evidence from other faithful believers in other denominations that a general rot was in progress. There is no doubt that the stand Spurgeon bravely took helped greatly to drive back the oncoming surge of Liberalism in the churches of the world. Evangelical Christianity is greatly indebted to the Banner of Truth Trust who published a number of works to keep what came to be called the Downgrade Controversy in memory as a fitting warning of what can always happen in churches who lose their First-love.

When we peruse the pages of the *Sword and Trowel* concerning the downgrading of Christian doctrine and witness, it becomes immediately clear that those downgrading issues

---

[20] *The Sword and the Trowel*, Oct. 1887, p. 512, Nov. 1887, p. 559

face us today as never before since Spurgeon's days. Spurgeon summed these issues up in his day in the words of Dr David Brown, Principal of the Free Church College, Aberdeen in *The Christian Age*. In the article quoted at length, Principal Brown examines the scepticism prevalent amongst former sound ministers which caused them 'to minimise all those features of the gospel which the natural man cannot receive.' Indeed, they strove 'to naturalise as far as possible, everything in religion,' and to water down the definite work of the Atonement, teaching that Christ's 'sufferings are not held forth in their vicarious and expiatory character. Christ, according to their teaching, was in no sense our Substitute, and in justification the righteousness of the glorious Surety is not imputed to the guilty believer.'[21] Though many attempts both well-meaning and malignant were made to keep Spurgeon quiet on the issue, he looked back to the works of his mentor and predecessor John Gill to help him stem the tide. On 27 November, 1887 he wrote to his Co-Pastor and Deacons:

> I cannot, at this present, tell you what spite has been used against me, or you would wonder indeed; but the love of God first, and your love next, are my comfort and stay. We may, perhaps be made to feel some of the brunt of the battle in our various funds; but the Lord liveth. My eminent predecessor, Dr John Gill, was told by a certain member of his congregation who ought to have known better, that, if he published his book, *The Cause of God and Truth*, he would lose some of his best friends, and

---

[21] *Ibid*, Oct. 1887, p. 512.

> that his income would fall off. The doctor said, 'I can afford to be poor, but I cannot afford to injure my conscience:' and he has left his mantle as well as his chair in our vestry.[22]

Sadly now both Gill's and Spurgeon's testimony is being eroded by our modern evangelical, Reformed establishment, and especially John Gill's great book against Arminian Liberalism *The Cause of God and Truth* has been openly but not accurately criticized by such as Hulse and Iain Murray. Instead of evaluating the book for what it was intended to do and what it very ably did, Hulse and Murray feel free to criticize it because it did not foresee common-grace theology and did not recommended it.

The cuckoo's egg

Indeed, we see here that the Banner of Truth Trust, who formerly denounced the downgrading of the pure doctrines of grace, have sadly themselves now made a U-turn and joined the downgraders. This is made crystal clear in Issue 475 of the *Banner of Truth Magazine*. In an article entitled *Overcoming Hesitations about Evangelistic Preaching*, Hywel R. Jones claims that the former Reformed policy against mass Arminian crusades and the like, formerly shared by the BOT in the good old days of the nineteen fifties to seventies, 'went too far'[23]. The reason he gives is that 'there was an uncertainty about how election and evangelism could go together'. Jones goes

---

[22] *The Full Harvest*, Banner of Truth, p. 477.

[23] P. 17.

on to say, 'But now, with the sermons of Whitefield, Spurgeon and Lloyd-Jones, and biblical studies like the *Free Offer of the Gospel* by John Murray to point the way, there should be no lack of confidence and facility in this area.'

Here we see how subtly the so-called Banner of Truth lays the cuckoo's egg of doctrinal downgrading in the Reformed nest. Whitefield, Spurgeon and Lloyd-Jones were thoroughly Biblical on the scope of the atonement and on the unity of the will of God in the Trinity. Thus none of them dared or wished to substitute the full gospel which they preached for the teaching of a saviour for everybody based on the fairy tale of a salvation made for everyman on the basis of natural theology and natural law. Yet, under the disguise of Whitefield's, Spurgeon's and Lloyd-Jones' orthodoxy, they introduce the pagan gospel of a John Murray. He envisaged fallen natural man, influenced by fallen, natural theology, attaining to a perfect knowledge of salvation meted out by a god who was thrice in conflict with himself. In this cuckoo's egg, hatched in the warmth of hell, even this Everybody's Saviour is a saviour who cannot promise eternal salvation but admits that he has not the power to do what he wills. This is not overcoming hesitations about evangelistic preaching, it is refusing to preach evangelically in any form. It is giving poisonous stones for wholesome bread. Furthermore, the unevangelical evangelism of the other face of the Banner of Truth's Janus-like head is based on a most Liberal and pontifical critical rendering of the Bible text which ridicules the fixed and eternal Word of God. Thus a gospel without a fallen man, a trustworthy Christ, a sure and certain atonement and a Word of God which never becomes void is not a gospel at all. Any talk of preaching this gospel as a free offer to all is merely an attempt to leave the hearers in their chains of sin.

More than notion

The Banner of Truth Trust is quick to use Dr Martin Lloyd-Jones' name against any man of God with whom they are at the time in conflict. The testimony of this distinguished saint is displayed as an ensign of orthodoxy under which the Banner fight their new fight. Yet often Lloyd-Jones' fervent witness is misused. This is especially seen in the way Lloyd-Jones is quoted in the Banner's battle to enforce common-grace theology on her adherents and thus destroy the testimony of such alleged Hyper-Calvinists and Antinomians as the Huntingtonians, i.e. those who were called to life by God's grace through the evangelical preaching of William Huntington.

The truth is that 'The Doctor' was very moved and impressed by the testimony of the Huntingtonians and was not ashamed to testify from his Westminster Chapel pulpit that the religion of these people was 'more than notion' and an understanding of it was of immense value to those who wished to serve God with heart and head. When Iain Murray wrote in Issue 378 that, in my enthusiasm for Huntington, I (thus?) denigrated his Christian contemporaries in all denominations, I pointed out to Mr Murray that the bulk of my writing was based on the sound theology of Huntington's contemporaries in all the major denominations and that I had contributed at least five lengthy articles to his magazine's pages on such stalwart contemporaries as William Cowper and John Newton. I also pointed out that in my book which he was criticizing, I had listed over thirty contemporary names of people in all the major denominations who soundly supported the teaching of William Huntington and a good number of them had been converted under his ministry. I also pointed out to Mr Murray that a number of these people, including painter-pastor James Bourne, had also been highly praised by Dr Lloyd-Jones in his Foreword to Mrs Alexander's excellent Zoar Publication book *More than Notion* which is a study-in-depth of Huntingtonian piety. Indeed, Lloyd-Jones had written:

> There are some books of which it can be said that to read them is an experience, and one is never the same again. The extracts out of the lives of these various people who came in varied ways to a saving knowledge of the Lord Jesus Christ are, at one and the same time, convicting and encouraging. Some were poor and ignorant, others well placed socially, and learned and cultured; but all came to the same glorious experience.
>
> In reading about them one is shown the vital difference between a head-knowledge of the Christian faith and a true heart experience.
>
> In recommending it to the congregation at Westminster Chapel on a Friday night I said that it should be made compulsory reading for all theologians especially, but it will prove valuable also to all who long for a vital Christian experience.
>
> Many who have read it as the result of my recommendation have testified to the blessing they have received. In one church known to me the reading of the book by one man led to a prayer meeting such as they had not experienced before.

In these superficial and confused days I thank God for a book such as this and pray that He may bless it to countless souls.

Downgrading the Trinity

Both Huntington and Spurgeon emphasized that the downgrading of their times was due to the decline in orthodox teaching upholding the unity of the Trinity. If a person was wrong on the Trinity, they argued, they could not possibly be right on anything else to do with the gospel. Nowadays, once more, the Trinity is being attacked from corners one would never have imagined forty years ago and this from a traditional pro-Spurgeonic corner. Recent attacks on the unity of the Trinity by David Gay in the Banner of Truth magazine and in the John Murray reprint *The Free Offer of the Gospel*, have shown clear Socinian trends. Dr R. T. Beckwith, former Warden of Latimer House, Oxford and upholder of the truth in the Protestant Reformation Society has had the sad duty of censuring the Banner of Truth's own Prof. Paul Helm for coming far too close to Sabellianism in his selective minimising of the Biblical evidence. Of this 'regrettable development' in Helm's radical lecture given at the London Theological Seminary on 12 February, 2001, entitled *Cautious Trinitarianism* Dr Beckwith says, 'This negative development has involved an attenuation of Trinitarian doctrine and a reductionist approach to the biblical evidence on which it rests, and of these tendencies Professor Helm's lecture is a rather extreme example.'[24]

[24] See Beckwith's *The Calvinist Doctrine of the Trinity*, Harrison Trust, 2001.

This is all part of the modern trend which feels that any complex thinking is too difficult for normal believers so the gospel must be simplified and concentrated to suit modern 'quick-food' and 'easy-reader' needs. Sadly, purveyors of these spiritual junk-foodstuffs seem unable to think in a complex way themselves and in cutting down their gospel for their theological 'easy-readers', they cut out the basic essentials. The eternal sharing of a joint divine nature in the Trinity and the eternal, unchanging unity of will between Father, Son and Holy Spirit appears now to be a doctrine abandoned by our simplistic evangelical leaders. It is good to have modern Spurgeons such as Dr Beckwith still with us who can show us what the whole Bible and its whole gospel has to teach us where other teachers now strive to delude us. Not for nothing did William Huntington condemn the anti-trinitarian views of his natural law opponents. He told them to their face that getting the Trinity wrong was the start of getting everything wrong. Is this why the Banner of Truth has written so fiercely and wrongly against William Huntington?

Characteristics of the new downgrading

The Banner of Truth magazine's lengthy and intensive campaign to denigrate Huntington and Gill on common-grace grounds started with the anonymous onslaught on Huntington in the July, 1988 issue entitled *The Voice of Years*. Here, the taunts of long refuted heretics were revived and believed, challenging the very foundations and pillars of our reformed faith. Follow-up articles by Iain Murray, used the arguments of Robert Southey who had been hired by Murray the publisher to slander Huntington in the manner he had slandered John Newton, William Cowper and other saints. Lord Macaulay demonstrated that Southey was 'utterly destitute of the power of discerning truth from falsehood', yet Murray's namesake claims Southey's falsehood for his truth. This Banner of Truth material, culled uncritically and un-checked from unbelievers, accounts for the wildest historical errors, faulty quotes and misrepresentations in their anti-Huntington articles. The main Banner problems were Huntington's works themselves and biographer Thomas Wright who has given us such fine doctrinal portrayals of Huntington, Cowper, Toplady, Watts, Hart and Beddome. Throughout Murray's ill-prepared attack on Huntington's works, he gets author, recipients, source contents and teaching wrong, painstakingly confusing secondary accounts with primary sources. Wright, a Valiant for Truth on the Calvinist side, is denounced for his (better) use of sources and denigrated as an amateur theologian of low spiritual insight for his sturdier faith.

Teaching the law lawfully

Murray claims Huntington viewed the law as abolished, merely because he refused to believe that Sinai was the sole rule of faith for Christians. Huntington believed that the Mosaic Law revealed the eternal character of God and on the day of judgment, the Book would be taken out and mankind judged according to how he has kept the law. Law-breakers will be condemned but those for whom Christ has kept the law and have been imputed with Christ's righteousness shall be saved. This led Huntington to write a number of works against the Antinomians of his day who were mainly common-grace and

Sinai-bound pseudo-Calvinists. He pointed them to the law of Christ and the law of faith, showing how the Mosaic law condemns us but the laws of Christ and faith give life.

Huntington critics such as Hulse and Murray erroneously compare Huntington negatively with the Marrow Men as if he were their opposite, not realizing how close the old Coalheaver was to them. Huntington held the Marrow Men in great esteem and had an almost identical view to theirs in presenting Christ in the gospel and used the term 'offer' as they did, claiming that Christ offers Himself to those with whom He is in covenant. The Marrow Men were certainly not common-grace gospellers of the John Murray type and certainly stood much nearer to Huntington and Gill in their theology than Erroll Hulse and Iain Murray. This even Andrew Fuller saw and this was the reason why he criticized the Marrow Men. Modern common-grace enthusiasts thus understand neither their enemies nor their friends correctly.

Despising the poor working man

Murray affirms that Huntington's lack of education and humble background denied him the right to become a minister and own a coach. Yet, Murray's coach-driving mentors Andrew Fuller, John Newton, Thomas Scott and William Carey also had what we might call a 'deprived upbringing'. Iain Murray, himself, has an average academic background and was not born with a silver spoon in his mouth, so why does he disqualify Huntington because of *his* humble background and *his* use of a carriage? Mr Murray certainly drives around in better cars than many other ministers possess who cannot afford the relatively luxurious trans-world life he leads. Murray also obviously wishes to give the impression that Huntington was stupid and despised learning, claiming that he called books disdainfully 'dead men's brains'. The true story is that Huntington knew he badly needed books to educate himself but found them too expensive. One day, an anonymous correspondent told him that a number of 'dead men's brains' would soon arrive. They arrived in the form of two parcels of books, which were put to good use. Huntington's lengthy account of these gifts, one would think, can neither be misunderstood nor misinterpreted. Indeed, Mr Murray's lengthy and numerous attacks in writing against Huntington never give the impression that he has studied Huntington to any length at all but has merely taken up the criticisms of those who hardly knew Huntington themselves such as the author of *The Voice of Years*.

John Gill defamed

Another full-gospeller, John Gill, though learned, is sadly also denigrated by the common-grace movement. They claim that Gill's church shrunk and Fuller, their common-grace mentor, preached to a thousand and that Fuller's system caused a great revival and Gill's system died out with his death. John Rippon's and Charles H. Spurgeon's highly positive praise of Gill is turned round like the dead men's brains story, and negated, to 'prove' the very opposite. Actually, Gill filled his church to bursting, and it remained one of the very largest Baptist churches in Britain for over fifty years. Fuller's church never reached this size over any lengthy period, indeed Fuller ended his life on a very sad note, relating how his association churches were all shrinking under the 50 members mark though old-path churches were growing. Then and during the next decades men of various denomination such as Huntington, Hawker, Gadsby and Doudney were preaching to thousands. Fuller's Association was the first Particular Baptist Association to deny the inerrancy of God's Word whilst full-gospel preachers kept firmly anchored in the Scriptures and reaped fruit. The missionary enterprise these Fullerites set up, to Spurgeon's chagrin, became so void of theological content and Christian testimony that they opened up membership to anyone capable of paying the 10 shillings-a-year fee. There is no doubt whatsoever that Spurgeon saw such developments as part and parcel of the general downgrading of true religion.

Gill is depicted as not preaching repentance and faith to sinners. Rippon tells us that his whole ministry was devoted to preach repentance and faith to all men everywhere. Yet, Iain Murray, in his badly researched booklet *Spurgeon v. Hyper-Calvinism*, ransacks Rippon's highly positive biography of Gill to find words which he might turn clumsily to speak against Gill. These 'quotes' prove strained indeed.

Spurgeon takes up Gill's mantle

Spurgeon found much strength and support in Gill's works which he gave a 'distinguished place' in his library, calling them 'greatly prized', 'invaluable', and 'precious'. Referring to Gill's great work on the Song of Solomon, Spurgeon says that those who despise Gill's teaching have either never read him or they 'are incapable of elevated spiritual feeling.' Such incapabilities are demonstrated in Murray's attack on Gill, fully corroborating the maxim 'He stoops to conquer'. Murray claims Spurgeon is 'over-generous' to Gill and Rippon 'too peace loving' to criticise him. Quoting a work against hypothetical Hyper-Calvinism, Murray tells his reader falsely that it conveys Spurgeon's personal animosity to Gill, though it neither mentions Gill, nor describes Gill's theology, nor was it even authored by Spurgeon. Murray backs this up with a number of other misleading distortions, claiming they describe Gill's ministry, such as Gill's allegedly not inviting sinners to repent and believe, alleged unhistorical reasons for Gill drawing up his 1729 Declaration of Faith, his alleged nearness to Antinomianism etc., etc.. During these imaginary accounts, Murray uses John 5:20 to 'prove' that Gill denied human responsibility though Andrew Fuller and John Rippon used Gill's very exposition of this text to show that Gill clearly did teach human responsibility! When it comes to throwing stones, modern Fullerites quite outdo their mentor. Hence the term Hyper-Fullerite describes them the best.

Part 3: The Gospel Of Man's Agency

On human responsibility, repentance and faith

The weakest flaw in the defence of common-grace enthusiasts is their affirmation that they alone teach full human responsibility for sin. On the other hand, they claim that those traditional Calvinists whom they call 'Hypers' do not preach that man is responsible for his fallen state or is accountable for not accepting Christ. This is because they link their two-fold gospel of common grace and saving grace with their two-fold view of man as a natural and moral being. In their system, natural theology or common grace speaks to the natural man and saving grace speaks to moral man. Both parts of man are appealed to in the gospel but both parts are not like fallen. The results of the fall, according to Johnson, John Murray, Hulse and other common-gracers, are seen in man's moral being alone and not in his natural being and his inabilities are not natural inabilities but moral inabilities. Indeed, Fuller, himself denied that man was even unable morally to choose God but put it down to a mere moral reluctance on man's part.

Johnson, following most present-day Fullerites, defines man's fall as 'a moral defect' or 'moral inability', whereas John Gill saw every man jack in his entire being as 'blame-worthy' and 'criminal'.[25] In other words, the common-gracers seek to explain sin in psychological terms, as used in describing a person's psychological want of moral balance. Gill looked upon man's responsibility as a voluntary, designed breaking of God's law. Common-grace gospellers look upon sin as a sign that man does not go far enough. He could do better. The Scriptures look upon sin as a transgression of the law, viewing man thus as going too far in following his own agency. Our Reformers, followed by such as Gill went to the true heart of the matter and saw man as totally condemned by God for his rebellion against Him. God blames and condemns man for sinning. One can excuse 'defects' in humans, but not rebellion against God.

Sin does not divide human nature, nor does salvation

As common-grace enthusiasts follow Joseph Bellamy and Andrew Fuller in dividing human nature into the fallen morally and the naturally able, it is no wonder that they link up common grace with natural man. Did not Fuller himself argue that man is fully capable of seeing God's loving-kindness in creation and thus deducing that he is duty bound to accept all God's revelation from wherever it comes? Did not Bellamy argue that though man is fallen morally, he is still naturally able to keep all the Ten Commandments?[26] All he needs to do is allow his

---

[25] See Gill's 1729 Statement of Faith and *Cause of God and Truth*, Section XXX.

[26] See Bellamy's chapter 'All mankind are capable of perfect conformity to God's law' in his *True Religion Delineated.*

natural ability to get the better of his moral defect. He can if he wills it. Thus common grace is there to lead man naturally to belief which thus opens the door to his grasping out and utilising the saving provisions of God.

Gill always emphasized human responsibility for being a sinful Christ-denier, explaining in *On Repentance towards God*, that true evangelical repentance was not only a turning from sin but a turning to God and this message was a substantial part of the gospel to sinners. When commenting on Acts 2:37, 38 'Repent and be baptized, every one of you, for the remission of sins,' Gill says:

> And this is also clear from the ministry of Christ himself: who came, not to call the righteous, but sinners to repentance; which was not a legal, but evangelical repentance. He began his ministry thus; *Repent, and believe the gospel*; see Matthew 9:13; Mark 1:15. With which agrees the ministry of the apostles in general; who, by the direction of Christ, preached repentance and remission of sins in his name; which was most certainly the gospel; the one, as well as the other, a doctrine of the gospel, Luke 24:47. And the apostle Paul, who was a most evangelical preacher, divides his whole ministry into these two parts; Repentance towards God, and faith towards our Lord Jesus Christ, Acts 20:21.

Happily, a number of scholars are now vindicating Gill the evangelist. Comparing Gill's evangelical fervour favourably with that of Edwards and claiming that Gill exhorted sinners to faith at least as much as Fuller (which is not saying too much), Gregory A. Wills, in his essay *A Fire that Burns Within: The Spirituality of John Gill*, says, quoting Gill:

> Gill followed his own advice: he urged sinners to seek salvation ... He urged sinners to trust their souls to Christ: 'What though, poor soul, thou seest the aboundings of sin in thy nature, and in every power and faculty of thy soul; yet look upon and view the superabounding grace of God streaming through the person, blood, and righteousness of Christ;
>
> ... take heart, therefore, and do not be discouraged; Christ's grace is sufficient for thee; ... go to him as a poor perishing sinner, implore his grace, and venture on him, I dare say he will not reject thee.

Incapable of natural and theological discernment

Though John Rippon defends Gill on almost every complaint that Iain Murray brings up against him, Murray strives time and time again to give the very opposite impression. To do so, he claims that Rippon rejected Gill's 1729 statement of faith when he took over Gill's church. We are to infer that Rippon wanted a new start with a new theology. Nothing could be further from the truth. Rippon asked members to sign Gill's declaration as the standard of the church's belief well into the 19th century, over thirty years after taking over Gill's church. Indeed, he had the declaration reprinted for his church as late as 1800. Murray also denigrates Gill through highly edited and sifted quotes from Ivimey the Baptist historian, ignoring the fact that Ivimey is most positive in his overall comments on Gill, confessing with

Rippon that he 'preached in the fullness of the blessing of the gospel of Christ; enriched, and generally enriching.'

This modern downgrader's idea of Gill, stands in stark contrast to the contemporary information we have of the pastor's preaching and witness from the pen of John Rippon. Nowadays, such as Murray and Hulse wish to press Gill into an Antinomian and Hyper-Calvinist corner, quoting Rippon in their attempt to do so, whereas Rippon, quite in contrast, pointed out that so appealing was Gill's preaching that critical visitors thought he was an Arminian![27]

This shows how even leaders of the contemporary Reformed scene are totally incapable of understanding man's being and lack of theological discernment and have clearly left the Calvinist paths they proclaim that they tread. This was obviously true of Rippon's day, too, as he goes on to say of Gill's critics that they speak, 'not knowing what they say, not whereof they affirm.' This Rippon applies, accompanied by very strong words, to those who relate Gill to either Arminianism or Antinomianism. Rippon cannot understand how Gill could be attacked from both sides like this but he mentions that Christ was hung up between two robbers and Gill between the Arminian robbers who rob God of His grace and the Antinomian robbers who rob God of His glory.[28]

Defining sin as sin

Before me lies a Banner of Truth book entitled *No Holiness, No Heaven!* It has little indeed to say of holiness and next to

---

[27] *The Life of John Gill*, pp. 102, 103.

[28] *Ibid*, pp. 103, 104.

nothing about heaven but is a preaching up of the law and a preaching down of sovereign grace evangelists whom Richard Alderson, the author, calls Antinomians and worse. In the book, I read that we neglect to give man rightful due for his part in his own salvation and must take note of Philippians 2:12, 13 which shows 'The strength is God's but the resultant effort is ours.' This was quite a new interpretation to me which I can in no way recommend. I had known Richard for many years, visiting Westminster Chapel with him and had also attended his English classes to compare notes on teaching English to foreign students. We later corresponded with each other on a number of occasions on theology and teaching methods. At that time, I thought that we were one heart and one soul in fellowship and doctrine. Alderson's 'about turn' on matters of church history surprised me. Furthermore, in the book, without giving any evidence whatsoever apart from the fact that he believes his 'Antinomians' were too Christo-centric and not andro-centric enough, Alderson claims that such as Crisp and Romaine separate justification from sanctification. The hint appears to be that sanctification does not follow justification but gains it. Being fairly conversant with Crisp's *Christ Alone Exalted*, I was ill-prepared for what my friend had to say about the great work. In the copy of Crisp I possess, I had written that no other book apart from the Bible describes the glories of Christ's work like this one. No other book describes the vileness of man, even saved man, as this book does. Imagine my surprise, therefore, to read Alderson's words:

> Tobias Crisp, for example, in a Hyper-Calvinistic fit assures us that 'an elect person is not in a condemned

state while an unbeliever, and should he happen to die before God call him to believe, he would not be lost.' This piece of theological lunacy would cut the nerve of all evangelistic and missionary endeavour. If we may permit ourselves a play on words, it was all due to bias, Crisp.' (Tobias Crisp).

After this cheap display of quite unwarranted criticism, low humour and careless use of undocumented sources, Alderson then tells us, 'Tobias Crisp – whose heart was, we trust, better than his head – has mislead many into believing that Christians are sinless, like their Lord.'

This surmise on Alderson's part appears to be because Crisp believed that a Christian is not merely pardoned but is freed from guilt. Of course, common-gracers, on the whole, teach like the Arminians that in salvation, the sinner is pardoned but is still under the rule of the law which pronounces him ever guilty. They argue like this because, as Fuller, they have no love for the teaching that it is Christ's righteousness which saves us and not our own and in Christ we stand fully acquitted before God because of Christ's righteousness imputed to us. This they call 'inherent righteousness', not being able to discern between the Roman doctrine of human righteousness and that imputed by Christ. On this count, it is the common-grace gospellers who believe in the popish inherent righteousness as they follow Fuller in teaching that unfallen natural abilities can regulate man's moral lapses through what the old theologians called 'a legal work', their slogan being, 'We can if we will'. Thus in his essays on *Moral Inability* and *Reply to Mr Button*, Fuller argues that man is not totally fallen as he has the same moral powers to believe or not to believe as he had before the fall.[29]

Needless to say, after checking Crisp's works and also in subsequent correspondence and talks with Mr Alderson, several friends and myself found out that he had no personal knowledge of Crisp's works but had relied on 'quotes' borrowed from enemies of Crisp, who obviously do not appear to have been knowledgeable of Crisp either. Mr Alderson, assured me that he wished to warn people against the dangers of Antinomianism and felt that he had chosen a didactically acceptable way. My retort that he should then have chosen a real Antinomian as a subject, obviously came too late. After complaining that Alderson's book 'contains unsubstantiated quotations from Tobias Crisp's sermons that are nowhere to be found in his works', another writer said of Alderson's strategy:

> If a man is to write a polemic against men of greater spiritual standing and learning than himself, let him first be thoroughly acquainted with their writings before he undertakes the foul deed. 'Thinking' Christians today have a crisis of confidence in the accuracy and scholarship of modern religious authors. How can we trust modern 'Reformed' writers when their bias is so superficial and dishonestly revisionist?[30]

---

29 *Works*, III, p. 768; II, p. 438.

30 *Defamation Today,* from *A Sinner Saved* Summer 1999, p. 13.

Sometime before my correspondence with Mr Alderson on Crisp, which he had started by kindly sending me a copy of his book with a covering letter, I had a similar correspondence with the Banner of Truth editors regarding Huntington and Fuller concerning their numerous highly unbalanced articles. I was told on behalf of the magazine that no criticism of Huntington's person was intended in the articles but he was being used didactically to warn young Christians of certain pitfalls and Fuller was similarly used to show the other side. In our correspondence, I was cautioned for my 'immoderate' language because I had protested against the editors' and Robert Oliver's all too strong language against men of impeccable characters and belief. I was also told that I was 'unjust' to bring up evidence against Fuller 'as though it showed he was not a Calvinist' (sic!). Mr Murray accused me of being 'careless' in my complaint about his use of Southey to denigrate Huntington on two counts, a. neither he nor Robert Oliver had quoted a single fact that really depended on Southey and b. Mr Murray thought I would have agreed with Southey's low opinion of Huntington. One can only conclude that Mr Murray had merely used Southey as a piece of vicious gossip. Furthermore, Mr Murray knew me well enough from many years of regular and detailed correspondence that I could not possibly agree with Southey against Huntington, nor against any of the other 18th century stalwarts who were denigrated by Southey's tongue and pen. Here Murray was apparently claiming innocence of the fact that Southey pioneered unfounded criticism of Huntington as he did John Newton and that Murray was using this for his own unfounded critical purposes. Murray had, in fact, quoted Southey, with very obvious agreement, as saying that the Old Coalheaver, 'was a sort of Evangelical Ishmaelite, and in that character considered himself at war, not only with the Church, but with all sects and denominations.'[31] As if I should have agreed to that!

In the course of this correspondence, the Banner of Truth editor told me that his criticism of Huntington had nothing to do with Fuller's theology and that he had not looked in detail at points in Fuller's doctrine which were wrong. However, it was Mr Murray himself who had sent me an article by Fuller at the very beginning of his drawn-out campaign against Huntington which he alleged showed Huntington to be an Antinomian. I had pointed out to Mr Murray that Fuller confessed that he knew little of Huntington and had only peeped into his works at the beginning of the 19th century when Huntington was at the height of his power and Fuller's work was waning. His only interest in the saint was to cull material to 'prove' that Huntington, his great rival, was an Antinomian and therefore discredit him. Fuller, as his later writings show, just could not get used to the fact that he was losing his hundreds whereas Huntington was gaining thousands as never before. The now old, barren tree was envious of the old tree that bore the most fruit.

I also corresponded with Mr Murray's co-editor at the time, Maurice Roberts, who maintained that Fuller was 'one of the great theologians in England at this period,' yet confessed that he was unfamiliar with Fuller's works. When I challenged him on his strong criticisms of Huntington, I found that he had read but one small book of the saint's, *A Rule and the Riddle*

---

[31] Banner of Truth magazine, Issue 373, p. 18.

and had quite misunderstood the rule and had not been able to solve the riddle. On my asking Mr Roberts how he could conclude from such limited knowledge of Huntington that he was an Antinomian and therefore a man of low morals, Mr Roberts strove to dodge the issue by assuring me that he was not referring to Huntington's practical low moral conduct but merely to his theoretical low moral conduct. Yet anyone who has truly read and studied this work of Huntington's for spiritual profit and not merely to find theoretical objections, must be impressed with the high Scriptural morality shown in that work, whether we understand it in a practical way, as Huntington intended it to be understood, or in a theoretical way, whatever the latter may mean.

I have been recently strongly criticised in public in Canada and the States by a group of Baptist ministers who resent my views on Fuller, Gill and Huntington. As one of them had boasted at an after-dinner speech that he had not read the work he was openly criticizing in such speeches and in writing, I wrote to the gentleman asking for his explanation. Another pastor replied quickly, saying that he was an agent for the man to whom I had written, and claiming that I was an immoral man because of my criticism of Fuller.[32] I wrote back and asked this person what he knew of my books and those of Fuller's, Gill's and Huntington's. He replied most impudently telling me that he had not read a word of mine, Fuller's nor Gill's etc. but he 'was entitled to his opinion'! This is what we seekers after truth and righteousness are up against in this modern debate. Those

[32] The book referred to was my *Law and Gospel in the Theology of Andrew Fuller*, Go Publications, 1996.

who are against the faith of the Prophets, Apostles and Reformers are all froth and bubble and so often men of little study and fewer morals. We are being hoodwinked just as the 19th century Liberals tried to hoodwink and silence Spurgeon. Just recently, I received a letter from a person who had read an article of mine in a teacher's magazine defending the American Puritans against Arthur Miller's criticism. My correspondent called me a 'moron', telling me that it was legitimate to tell small lies in order that the greater truth should come out. Of course, I had addressed this point critically, too, in my vindication of Cotton Mather to which my critic referred. According to Puritan William Turner, this was the method of the Precisians and Rome in the Counter-Reformation and is the method Arthur Miller uses to sell his books. Have our Christian leaders of today fallen back into Precisian, Roman and dramaturgical cheating, doing evil so that that good might come of it? If so, we believers at the grass roots must be on our guard indeed.

Coming back to Richard Alderson, I presume that the collectors of quotes and comment he used, as he gives no direct sources, were thinking of the dialogue on the covenant of free grace and the timing of justification in Crisp's sermon entitled *The New Covenant of Free Grace*. Crisp is arguing against the faulty idea that justification is a product of human faith. In the immediate context, he is answering the question, 'Is not faith here the condition of the covenant?' To which Crisp answers:

> There is no person under heaven shall be saved till he hath believed. This I grant; yet this will not make faith to

> be the condition of the covenant. For, first, consider faith as an act, our act, and as we do it, so I say, it is a work; our act of believing is a work. If therefore, we perform the condition that is a work for the enjoyment of the covenant, then the covenant doth depend upon a work; but it doth not depend upon a work, for the text saith, 'To him that worketh not, but believeth on him that justifieth the ungodly.[33]

Crisp goes on to argue that justification of the ungodly must come before belief, otherwise it would be justification of the godly, but we are justified whilst at enmity with God. Christ justifies alone but in justifying the ungodly, he gives them faith.

Similarly, Alderson has done no justice to Crisp or to the gospel in striving to understand – and warp – his view of sin. Crisp shocked a number of fellow clergymen because he taught that even in acts of faith believers still sin. In other words, he taught the exact opposite of Alderson's gossip. In the work Alderson purports to quote second hand, Crisp says:

> In one word, beloved, mistake me not, I am far from imagining any believer is freed from acts of sin; he is freed only from the charge of sin; that is, from being a subject to be charged with sin; all his sins are charged upon Christ, he being made sin for him, yet Christ is not an actual sinner; but Christ is all the sinners in the world by imputation; and through this imputation all our sins are so

---

33 *The Sermons of Tobias Crisp*, Tobias Crisp Series, Issue 2, Christian Bookshop, Ossett p. 32.

> done away from us, that we stand as Christ's own person did stand, and doth stand in the sight of God. Now, had not Christ made a full satisfaction to the Father, he himself must have perished under those sins that he did bear; but in that he went through the thing, and paid the full price, as he carried them away from us, so he laid them down for himself. So that now Christ is freed from sin, and we are freed from sin in him; he was freed from sin imputed to him and laid upon him, when he suffered; we were freed from sin as he takes it off from our shoulders, and hath carried it away; 'Come unto me all ye that are weary and heavy laden.' That is, with sin. And what follows? 'And I will give you rest.' As long as the burthen is upon his shoulders, so long there is no rest. Therefore this doth necessarily import, that Christ must take away the burthen, that we may have rest.[34]

Crisp's *Christ Alone Exalted* has two volumes full of this exquisite preaching of the full gospel to all men. No blasphemous preaching of God doing His bit and man's doing his or weird tales of salvation being all God's work but also all the work of man can be a substitute for or supplement to Crisp's golden-tongued preaching. Who wants the cheap imitation of the Banner's *No Holiness, No Heaven!* when the doctrine revealed in the book is that holiness which comes from keeping the law of Sinai. That mountain only brought damnation on man, *Christ Alone Exalted* brought that salvation which we are commissioned by our Saviour to

---

[34] *Ibid,* Issue 1, p. 15.

preach to all nations. William Twisse, first Moderator of the Westminster Assembly, is still correct concerning Crisp. He said that he was so much criticised because he put other ministers to shame by winning so many souls for Christ and they had little to show for their preaching. Over half of the modern common-gracers I know look back on great pastoral troubles in a number of tiny churches that soon grew tired of them. Yet these spiritual gnats never lose their appetite for biting spiritual giants like Gill, Huntington and Crisp to boost their own ego.

Common grace linked to man's supposed agency

Erroll Hulse claims that it is the disagreement over man's ability or disability to exercise responsibility in matters of salvation which is 'the root of the matter and the reason why it is necessary to be clear about common grace'.[35] This grace, Hulse argues, finds man quite able to exercise responsibility and accountability before God and be reasoned with and addressed by Him. He thus recommends Spurgeon's sermon on Isaiah 1:18 in which the great preacher allegedly summons his hearers on the grounds of common grace to be reasonable and wise and thus believe and live.[36]

On turning to Spurgeon's full exposition of this sermon, which Hulse has strangely misapplied, one finds quite another story. Spurgeon is not approaching sinners through common-grace but using the picture of the fishermen who cast out their nets, calling on Father, Son and Holy Ghost to provide the catch. Furthermore, Spurgeon's topic is the wisdom, grace

[35] *The Free Offer*, p. 15.
[36] *Ibid*, p. 15 ff.

and power of God and not man's agency. Of man, Spurgeon says that sinners are not *sensible*[37] to God, indeed, Spurgeon calls then *senseless*. He condemns them in God's Name as being not only *deaf* to God and *worse than beasts* but *totally dead* to God's appeals. In other words, Spurgeon behaves as one of Curt Daniel's and Hulse's 'Hypers' and preaches almost verbatim like Gill! Hulse's strategy, totally unfair to Spurgeon, is also used in Iain Murray's booklet *Spurgeon v. Hyper-Calvinism*. This highly selective, unfair presenting of Spurgeon has caused many to turn their backs on the Prince of Preachers. After the Murray debacle on Spurgeon, some common-grace pastors, who wished to present Spurgeon to the German public as a nigh Arminian, approached me for help. I offered them Spurgeon's great work *All of Grace* in German. I was quickly told there was no interest in such a publication. After Murray's thoroughly unbalanced presentation of Spurgeon, his 'Calvinistic' side was not wanted. I was told it was not representative of the great Baptist! Obviously, in this modern downgrading of our Christian faith, it is strategically 'sound' to downgrade the theology of the one who stood foremost against the sad downgrading of his own day.

Dead but yet alive!

The idea that man is not dead in trespasses and sins can be

---

[37] The use of the term 'sensible' concerning the Spirit's application of the Word on the sinner is a sure sign of 'Antinomianism' for modern Fullerites. They forget that Bunyan, Hervey, Fuller, Spurgeon, Gill and many other evangelists looked to the Spirit to make man 'sensible' of the gospel. Surely this has nothing whatsoever to do with Antinomianism!

traced back to the high view of post-fall man expressed by Moral Governmentalists such as New Divinity author Joseph Bellamy.[38] They insist, because of their probationist views, that if man were totally fallen both naturally and morally and thus totally dead in trespasses and sins, as Gill, Huntington and Spurgeon taught, he could not be held responsible for his state. They have come too late with such judgment. God beat them to it when he condemned probationer Adam for his failure! Orthodoxy has always maintained that God has condemned and rejected fallen man because he is responsible for his sin – but not for his salvation! His death is his own responsibility. God does not punish a dead man, death is the punishment itself. Thus when the common-gracers tell us that every man has the ability to reason with God and if he could not, God would be unjust, they are striving to reverse the fall and their argument is totally invalid. This is one gospel truth that Fuller just would not accept. Arguing that only reluctance and aversion separates us from God, and man has the same powers to believe as not to believe, Fuller claims:

> If the inability of sinners to believe in Christ were of the same nature as that of a dead body in a grave to rise up and walk, it were absurd to suppose that they would on this account fall under the divine censure. No man is reproved for not doing that which is naturally impossible.[39]

[38] See Michael Haykin's *One Heart and One Soul* for Bellamy's vast influence on the Fullerite School.
[39] *Works*, Vol. II, pp. 355-357.

Fuller thus believed that fallen man has all his natural abilities intact, making him still eligible for salvation by virtue of his nature. Here Fuller is reviving the 'probation' or 'second chance' theory of the New Divinity school, taught by Bellamy in his Author's Preface to *True Religion Delineated*, the book which influenced Fuller the most:

> We are designed, by God our Maker, for an endless existence. In this present life we just enter upon being, and are in a state introductory to a never-ending duration in another world, where we are to be forever unspeakably happy or miserable, according to our present conduct. This is designed for a state of probation, and that for a state of rewards and punishment. We are now upon trial, and God's eye is upon us every moment; and that picture of ourselves, which we exhibit in our conduct, the whole of it taken together, will give our proper character, and determine our state forever.[40]

Taking God's command 'Thou shalt love the Lord thy God with all thy heart', Bellamy develops his gospel of probationary duties based on God's moral government which he calls Divine Law. Bellamy speaks of Divine Law as revealed through nature, Moses and the gospel, seeing a progression in man's dutiful and saving awareness of God. Thus to recognize one's duties to God in nature is to recognize one's duties to God in His law and this leads one on to recognize one's duties to God in the gospel. Bellamy outlines

---

[40] *Op. cit.* p. 52.

the gospel as: '1. The duty required – Love to God. 2. The grounds and reasons of duty intimated – Because he is the Lord our God. 3. The measure of duty required – With all thy heart.' For Bellamy, the gospel describes these duties to men in the form of moral laws to prevent man from falling. He does not want man to make the same mistake as Adam. Here again, the common-gracers have come too late with their law-bound teaching. Mankind was on probation in Adam and failed. Since then, everyman has made the same mistake as Adam. No one is in a state of probation. All are in a state of damnation unless God intervenes. God will not allow us to make the same mistake twice. Thus we believers in the doctrines of grace welcome the gospel that is all of grace and not of law duty as the only grounds of our salvation. Daniel, Hulse and Murray all claim that those who reject their common-grace based free offer and their law-bound gospel of duty faith are Antinomians and Hypers. It is high time for orthodox Christians to turn the gospel tables on these people who put the law to its wrong use and reveal them to be the deluded Hyper-Antinomians they are.

No foundation for Hulse's gospel

Erroll Hulse professes to trace the common-grace gospel back to John Calvin. It is essential for him to do so in order to establish his common-grace gospel as 'Evangelical Calvinism' or 'Spurgeonic Calvinism', which is really no Calvinism at all. As long as Hulse can keep up a semblance of Calvinism, he is sure to find some Reformed people unused to thinking problems out for themselves who will back him. He argues therefore that his theory is not a half-way house between

Arminianism and Calvinism but a 'whole stop at Calvin's house'.[41] Without copious backing from Calvin, Hulse obviously feels, his arguments will all fall flat. What Hulse has forgotten to do is to provide even a fraction of this necessary copious evidence needed from Calvin's works. The *one* faulty source Hulse gives features *two* part-sentences from two works separated by 95 pages, both referring to the grace of God offered to the elect. It is well-known that Calvin neither wrote on, nor appealed to such an entity as 'common grace' as a basis for gospel preaching. Nor did he even mention the term more than two or three times in his entire works, let alone used it in the sense Hulse does. Why then does Hulse state so dogmatically that 'The doctrine of Common Grace was first expounded by John Calvin'?[42] The Banner's own Louis Berkhof tells us in his chapter on the subject in his *Systematic Theology* that the term 'cannot be said to owe its origin to Calvin'.[43] The answer to this question is that Berkhof is speaking of common grace as a 'communal grace', whose existence is a matter of doubt but which 'does not effect the salvation of sinners.' This is where he would place Calvin's attitude to what became known as common grace. Hulse is talking about a common grace that Calvin never refers to. Hulse's common grace helps, according to him, to effect salvation. Hulse also links common grace with what he calls the free offer of the gospel, indeed, he affirms that:

---

41 *Free Offer*, p. 14. The one quote Hulse gives from Calvin is spurious.
42 *The Free Offer*, p. 22.
43 See the chapter on Common Grace in Berkhof's *Systematic Theology*.

> the subject of common grace is inescapably connected with the free offer. It is not possible to deal adequately with the question of the offer without getting to grips with the subject of common grace.[44]

This was never Calvin's position. Calvin, as Gill, believed in an external call irrespective of God's normal dealings with nature. They did not confuse nature with grace. So when Hulse comes up with his sole undocumented quote from Calvin, 'The mercy of God is offered equally to those who believe and to those who believe not', using it to link up common grace and his free-offer gospel, he is placing it in a discussion quite foreign to Calvin's teaching.

Furthermore, Hulse neither tells us where Calvin wrote this, nor the context in which he wrote it, nor does he explain how this quote has anything to do with communal grace.

Calvin's and Edward's wayward offspring

Admittedly, Calvin is easily misunderstood by me or anyone else. Interpreters are of two minds on Calvin's Calvinism. Berkhof thinks Calvin is a Supralapsarian,[45] a term Curt Daniel uses to describe a Hyper-Calvinist. Alan Clifford writes profusely to prove that Calvin was an Amyraldian which one might think is the opposite of a Calvinist! I personally feel that Calvin, useful as he was to God in particular circumstances, fell short of such as Martin Bucer, Henry Bullinger, John Gill and many an English Reformer as an all-round pastoral theologian. Calvin

---

44 *Free Offer*, pp. 4, 5.
45 *Systematic Theology*, p. 118.

was always critical, even jealously so, of his mentors and put himself above them. He told Bucer, 'You are a man of peace but I am a man of truth.' In doing so, he forgot that he had his truth from Bucer, the man of peace and other Strasburg Reformers, often verbatim, (see the *Institutes*). Sadly, Calvin's jealousy of Valerand Poullain who had also been his mentor and fellow pastor caused him to travel to Frankfurt when newcomers started troubling the church. He persuaded the city authorities to drum his rival out of his refugee church which had kept true to him in France, England and Germany, and had Poullain robbed of all citizen's rights. His duplicity in first encouraging the Knoxian minority to stir up trouble at Frankfurt only to denounce them to Lord Burleigh and Elizabeth soon afterwards, is also well-recorded. History does not forget these incidents. Furthermore, Calvin, like Jonathan Edwards, though he kept within acceptable bounds of speculation himself, had successors who went way beyond his reasoning. Thus Calvin's speculative ideas of the Trinity, though perhaps harmless in themselves, provided others with a platform on which to erect Sabellianism. Edwards' highly speculative philosophy regarding the natural and moral capacities of man, has been made the platform on which modern common-grace enthusiasts erect a new teaching of the fall, atonement and salvation. Here Edwards is the more blameworthy, however, as Calvin could not have foreseen what Paul Helm was to make of his speculations but Edwards actually encouraged Bellamy personally to develop his moral-natural, dual nature theory of man and did not interfere when Bellamy totally exaggerated the difference and drew conclusions from it which stood orthodox Christianity on its head and eventually provided us with the curse of modern mass evangelism on a Finneyite basis. In other words, Calvin, good as he is, cannot possibly be our yardstick of orthodoxy, though we might find him the next best thing. Nor can Jonathan Edwards be the standard that modern Fullerites claim he is.

It is through taking Edward's thoughts, however, rather than Calvin's, to their logical conclusions that has determined the way much of our modern allegedly Reformed Establishment is going. Edwards paved the way for abandoning the penal doctrine of atonement and justification through denying their absolute essentiality and necessity. God, according to Edwards, could not only have used other ways to atone for sin and render a sinner right with God but the atonement itself had no essentiality in the sense that Christ actually experienced the wrath of God on our behalf.[46] For Edwards, this was a mere 'as if' demonstration or, to use the terminology of modern Fullerites, a *pro forma* act. If Christ knew all along that the atonement was merely a masquerade, why did Christ call out 'My God, My God. Why hast Thou forsaken me?' Was this, too, merely part of the 'as if' act? Here we see the developing doctrine of Socinius and Grotius which came to full bloom in Fullerism. They taught that God's will is wholly arbitrary, free of the necessity to which His own standards bind Him. In Him there is thus nothing absolute and especially no absolute justice and mercy. Thus, in the atonement, we have no penal satisfaction and no vicarious suffering but merely a demonstration to move man morally to look to God

---

[46] See Edwards' argument in his *Concerning the Necessity and Reasonableness of the Christian Doctrine of Satisfaction for Sin.*

or to move man governmentally to place himself under God's sovereignty. It was the teaching of John Gill, assisted by such as Augustus Toplady and John Ryland senior who brought back the Reformed teaching of the essentiality, necessity and reality of the atonement, imputed righteousness and justification. It is these three doctrines which are the major stumbling block to our common-grace gospellers as each for them are 'pro forma' and not real. Actually, if we are to follow the doctrines of these people, we abandon Christianity and merely play the game that cyberspace enthusiasts call 'virtual reality' which is the very opposite to the real thing.

The common-gracer's misuse of Calvin

Returning to Calvin, I am not saying that he never said the words Hulse quotes, but would have been thankful if Hulse had told his readers where he had found them and in what context. After spending many hours going through my CD versions of Calvin's commentaries, sermons, writings, Institutes etc. and the books by him in my possession, though I found Calvin promising, and in one case offering the mercy of God to those who were confessing their sins and hungering and thirsting after righteousness, I found nothing approaching Hulse's 'quote'. I did find that Calvin says, 'The covenant of life is not preached equally to all, and among those to whom it is preached, does not always meet with the same reception.'[47]

The fact is that Calvin speaks repeatedly against a universal offer of salvation and affirms that he recognizes solely an effectual call in the gospel because:

---

[47] *Institutes*, Vol. 2, Book III, p. 202.

> his mercy is offered to all who desire and implore it, and this none do, save those whom he has enlightened. Moreover, he enlightens those whom he has predestinated to salvation.[48]

Indeed, Calvin goes so far as to say that preachers do not call all equally and adds:

> Whence it is evident that the doctrine of salvation, which is said to be set apart for the sons of the Church only, is abused when it is represented as effectually available to all.[49]

Concerning those who argue that God wishes all men to be saved, irrespective of what God has decreed, Calvin, in his fifty-sixth lecture on Ezekiel, puts them right in explaining who the 'all' are and criticizes his opponents for giving the wishes of God two different meanings. God always wishes the same thing, Calvin explains, and always does what He wishes. Here Calvin is teaching that new men in Christ are new creations and such are those who God saves. All those whom He turns will, indeed, come to Him and be saved. He thus says:

> Since, therefore, repentance is a kind of second creation, it follows that it is not in man's power; and if it is equally in God's power to convert men as well as to

---

48 *Ibid*, p. 256.
49 *Ibid*, p. 222.

> create them, it follows that the reprobate are not converted, because God does not wish their conversion; for if he wished it, he would do it; and hence it appears that he does not wish it.

Calvin goes on to say that 'God rejects no returning sinner: he pardons all without exception.' This is the gospel Calvin preached to all, trusting that the Holy Spirit would turn His own. To equate this with an imaginary common grace which points to saving grace for all and claims Calvin as its perpetrator has no basis in either Scripture, history, logic or fair play. If common-gracers are faithful to their system and honest with their opponents, they are bound to call Calvin a Hyper-Calvinist. In other words, those common-gracers who hide under Calvin's Geneva gown are charlatans, serving under a false banner, bound on a false course to the Pelagian Islands of Never-Never Land. Such spiritual piracy is condemned in the Scriptures by both law and grace and will reap what it deserves.

Building on historical revisionism

Hulse makes much of Abraham Kuyper's three-volumed work on common grace *Gemeene Gratie* as a source of his theory and indeed, as we know from other statements of Hulse, he sees himself as treading in the footsteps of the famous Dutch politician and theologian. However, Hulse makes it very difficult for his readers to examine Kuyper at first hand and thus check Hulse's interpretation. Instead of telling us what Kuyper really says in English, Hulse tells us, apparently with his tongue in his cheek, that if we cannot read Dutch, we cannot benefit from

Kuyper's works. Should we look for an alternative in English, Hulse recommends another Dutch work, available in English, but again to dampen our enthusiasm, if not to put us off the track, Hulse tells us that the recommended work is far from clear and badly translated.[50] So the English reader is rather handicapped in scrutinizing Hulse's sources. We are furthermore told, also without evidence, that Bavinck, Warfield, Hodge and Calvin support Hulse.

Though Hulse is a South African Boer, he must have forgotten his childhood language as both Kuyper and Bavinck[51] make it quite clear in their original works that common grace is merely what it professes to be, a providential, natural grace common to all men. They also make it very clear indeed that common grace has nothing whatsoever to do with saving grace, free offers, duty faith etc.. If Hulse can prove that one of the 700 churches that Kuyper established had a common-grace based Declaration of Faith or any one of his 100 books taught such an error, Hulse will have my sincere apologies for missing what is totally hidden. But though Kuyper or an angel from heaven tells me that common grace is the same as saving grace, I would not forfeit my salvation to believe such an error simply because it titivates man's all too high an opinion of himself. Although I think that Kuyper, in seeking to revive views of nature long discarded by our Reformers, was doing no one a service, he certainly had a very fine and Scriptural view of saving grace. Neither Kuyper, Calvin, Charles Hodge nor

---

[50] *The Free Offer*, p. 22.

[51] If Hulse is referring to Bavinck's *De Algemeene Genade*, this work, as Kuyper's *Gemeene Gratie* merely refers to man's status, calling and function in nature and not in salvation.

Warfield, whom Hulse says back him, take off on Hulse's flight of fancy in claiming that saving grace is merely common grace pronounced differently.

A make-shift misuse of John Owen

The only solid source quote Hulse gives his readers to prove the historical standing of his common-grace theory is in a footnote referring to John Owen's work on Hebrews 6:4-6 for which we are provided with volume and page. However, Hulse, though he quotes Owen to back him up in the body of his essay, here says that Owen only 'comes close' to the common grace idea. However, even if Hulse could produce someone of note who even came near him in some degree, it would be interesting to study his evidence as most of the scholars Hulse quotes to back him up have quite different convictions to his. The proof of the pudding is in the eating, so we must turn to Owen's actual words. Hebrews 6:4-6 is the difficult passage concerning those who have met with God and become partakers of the Holy Ghost, yet have left Him and now cannot repent and find a way back to Him. This hardly 'comes close' to common grace, or saving grace, for that matter. Of these verses Owen says:

> Where there is a total neglect of the due improvement of this privilege and mercy, the condition of such persons is hazardous, as inclining towards apostasy. Thus much lies open and manifest in the text. But that we may more particularly discover the nature of this first part of the character of apostates, for their sakes who may look after their own concernment therein, we may yet a little

more distinctly express the nature of that illumination and knowledge which is ascribed unto them; and how it is lost in apostasy will afterwards appear. And, —

(1.) There is a knowledge of spiritual things that is purely natural and disciplinary, attainable and attained without any especial aid or assistance of the Holy Ghost. As this is evident in common experience, so especially among such as, casting themselves on the study of spiritual things, are yet utter strangers unto all spiritual gifts. Some knowledge of the Scripture, and the things contained in it, is attainable at the same rate of pains and study with that of any other art or science.

(2.) The illumination intended, being a gift of the Holy Ghost, differs from, and is exalted above this knowledge that is purely natural; for it makes nearer approaches unto the light of spiritual things in their own nature than the other doth. Notwithstanding the utmost improvement of scientifical notions that are purely natural, the things of the gospel, in their own nature, are not only unsuited to the wills and affections of persons endued with them, but are really foolishness unto their minds. And as unto that goodness and excellency which give desirableness unto spiritual things, this knowledge discovers so little of them, that most men hate the things which they profess to believe. But this spiritual illumination gives the mind some satisfaction, with delight and joy, in the things that are known. By that beam whereby it shines into darkness, although it be not fully comprehended, yet it represents the way of the gospel as a way of righteousness, 2 Peter 2:21, which reflects peculiar regard of it on the mind.

Moreover, the knowledge that is merely natural hath little or no power upon the soul, either to keep it from sin or to constrain it unto obedience. There is not a more secure and profligate generation of sinners in the world than those who are under the sole conduct of it. But the illumination here intended is attended with efficacy, and doth effectually press in the conscience and whole soul unto an abstinence from sin, and the performance of all known duties. Hence persons under the power of it and its convictions do ofttimes walk blamelessly and uprightly in the world, so as not with the other to contribute unto the contempt of Christianity.

Besides, there is such an alliance between spiritual gifts, that where any one of them doth reside, it hath assuredly others accompanying of it, or one way or other belonging unto its train, as is manifest in this place. Even a single talent is made up of many pounds. But the light and knowledge which is of a mere natural acquirement is solitary, destitute of the society and countenance of any spiritual gift whatever. And these things are exemplified unto common observation every day.

(3.) There is a saving, sanctifying light and knowledge, which this spiritual illumination riseth not up unto; for though it transiently affects the mind with some glances of the beauty, glory, and excellency of spiritual things, yet it doth not give that direct, steady, intuitive insight into them which is obtained by grace, 2 Corinthians 2:18, 4:4, 6. Neither doth it renew, change, or transform the soul into a conformity unto the things known, by planting of them in the will and affections, as a gracious saving light doth, 2 Corinthians 2:18; Romans 6:17, 12:2.

These things I judged necessary to be added, to clear the nature of the first character of apostates.

Owen's position is nowhere near Hulse's

Owen cannot be speaking in Hulsean terms here by any stretch of the imagination. Indeed, when he speaks of grace, which these apostates have not received, it is the grace which saves, not a grace which is common. Rather than speak about a common grace, Owen speaks about particular enlightenment which stops short of giving spiritual insight and transforming the soul.

Furthermore, Owen goes on to emphasise that he is not speaking of common gifts to all men but special gifts of the mind to special people who, nevertheless do not receive saving graces. The man with the least grace, he argues, is better off than the man with the greatest abundance of these special, God-given privileges and talents. It is interesting to note that Owen has a good deal to say about common sense in these expositions, but nothing anywhere near approaching common grace.

Owen and the Universalists

Hulse and his fellow Baptists argue that their Fullerite view of the atonement is the historic Particular or Reformed Baptist view (called Regular Baptist in the USA), but James P. Boyce, a Regular Baptist of note himself, shows how this is a most erroneous assumption.[52] Explaining in his famous *Abstract of Theology* how Fuller broke from the traditional Calvinistic concept of the Atonement, Boyce expounds at length how Fullerism must be placed in the category 'Universalism'. He criticizes Fuller for teaching:

> The work of the atonement had nothing to do with the persons to whom it was applied considered as an atonement, but only had respect to men as guilty sinners in God's sight. The work to be accomplished was precisely what would have been, had there been no election, no church to be established, no work of grace to be wrought on the heart, but each person left to act in its reception, or rejection, as he should choose.

Boyce demonstrates that the error of Fuller, which is continued by Hulse and his fellow common-grace gospellers, 'does not include the sovereign pleasure of God in the purpose to apply.' Thus, though Hulse and his faction speak of atonement, election, redemption, reconciliation, or any of the doctrines of grace, they are made such on the sinner's grasping out and taking them. This is election through reception and not the theology of the Bible and most certainly not the theology of Calvin. This is perhaps the major criticism of the entire so-called 'Evangelical Calvinism' movement. It is neither evangelical, as it destroys the Biblical 'evangel' or

---

[52] It may be argued that Boyce was a Southern Baptist and not Regular Baptist but the first term refers to the denomination and the second to the doctrines believed. See Chapter XXVII: The Atonement of Christ in Boyce's *Abstract*, especially p. 312 ff., 317 and 338.

gospel and it can by no means be called Calvinism as it destroys each and every doctrine of grace. Take away the falsely assumed title of 'Calvinist' from these people and all they have left is a heretical and superstitious sect.

Hulse quotes Owen as his ally but Fuller had also misunderstood Owen before Hulse took up the thread, thinking that the great Congregationalist believed in a universal atonement sufficient for all, though only applicable to those who grasped out and took it. In his great work *The Death of Death in the Death of Christ*, Owen goes to verbal war against all the different kinds of Universalists, alias common-grace gospellers, showing that their much emphasized 'alls', 'anys' and 'everys' should be studied in their individual context and not explained by an external theory. In Book IV, Owen gives a fine example of how such as Hulse and the Murrays argue against the true meaning of Scripture. Though Hulse, in his *The Free Offer* argues that 2 Peter 3:9 refers to the goodness of God to all men and Murray in his *The Free Offer of the Gospel* alters the text to prove that God wishes to save all men, Owen says:

> 2 Peter 3:9, 'The Lord is long-suffering to us-ward, not willing that any should perish, but that all should come to repentance.' 'The will of God,' say some, 'for the salvation of all, is here set down both negatively, that he would not have any perish, and positively, that he would have all come to repentance; now, seeing there is no coming to repentance nor escaping destruction, but only by the blood of Christ, it is manifest that that blood was shed for all.'

Ans. Many words need not be spent in answer to this objection, wrested from the misunderstanding and palpable corrupting of the sense of these words of the apostle. That indefinite and general expressions are to be interpreted in an answerable proportion to the things whereof they are affirmed, is a rule in the opening of the Scripture. See, then, of whom the apostle is here speaking. 'The Lord', saith he, 'is long-suffering to usward, not willing that any should perish.' Will not common sense teach us that us is to be repeated in both the following clauses, to make them up complete and full, — namely, 'Not willing that any of us should perish, but that all of us should come to repentance?' Now, who are these of whom the apostle speaks, to whom he writes? Such as had received 'great and precious promises', 2 Peter 1:4, whom he calls 'beloved', 2 Peter 3:1; whom he opposeth to the 'scoffers' of the 'last days', 2 Peter 3:3; to whom the Lord hath respect in the disposal of these days; who are said to be 'elect', Matthew 24:22. Now, truly, to argue that because God would have none of those to perish, but all of them to come to repentance, therefore he hath the same will and mind towards all and everyone in the world (even those to whom he never makes known his will, nor ever calls to repentance, if they never once hear of his way of salvation), comes not much short of extreme madness and folly. Neither is it of any weight to the contrary, that they were not all elect to whom Peter wrote: for in the judgment of charity he esteemed them so, desiring them 'to give all diligence to make their calling

> and election sure', 2 Peter 1:10; even as he expressly calleth those to whom he wrote his former epistle, 'elect', 2 Peter 1:2, and a 'chosen generation', as well as a 'purchased people', 2 Peter 2:9. I shall not need add anything concerning the contradictions and inextricable difficulties wherewith the opposite interpretation is accompanied (as, that God should will such to come to repentance as he cuts off in their infancy out of the covenant, such as he hateth from eternity, from whom he hideth the means of grace, to whom he will not give repentance, and yet knoweth that it is utterly impossible they should have it without his bestowing). The text is clear, that it is all and only the elect whom he would not have to perish.

Owen on 2 Peter 3:9 is crystal clear. His exegesis totally refutes that of Hulse, the Murrays and Phillip Johnson. Just as they really ought to call Calvin a Hyper-Calvinist, to be honest with themselves and consistent with their own theological notions, they ought to call Owen one, too. Indeed, they ought to call all our Reformers and Puritans 'Hypers' as their teaching opposed common-grace theology which smacks of the Mediaeval fantasies of Abelard.

Turning to the Westminster Confession for help

Our common-gracers always call the Westminster Confession to their defence yet in the article on *Effectual Calling*, the authors draw a firm line between what God's Providence provides and what grace accomplishes. In Section 4, the Confession states:

> Others, not elected, though they may be called by the ministry of the word, and may have some common operations of the Spirit, yet they never truly come to Christ, and therefore cannot be saved: much less can men, not professing the Christian religion, be saved in any other way whatsoever, be they never so diligent to frame their lives according to the light of nature, and the law of that religion they do profess; and to assert and maintain that they may is without warrant of the word of God.[53]

Boyce, too, has a bone to pick with the election-on-reception Reductionalists of the Fullerite school. He quotes from the Westminster Confession, Chapter 8 on *Christ the Mediator*, using Hodge's commentary:

> 5. The Lord Jesus, by His perfect obedience, and sacrifice of Himself, which He through the eternal Spirit, once offered up unto God, hath fully satisfied the justice of His Father; (Rom. 5:19, Heb. 9:14, 16, Heb. 10:14, Eph. 5:2, Rom. 3:25–26) and purchased, *not only reconciliation, but an everlasting inheritance in the kingdom of heaven, for all those whom the Father hath given unto Him.* (Dan. 9:24, 26, Col. 1:19–20, Eph. 1:11, 14, John 17:2, Heb. 9:12, 15).

[53] See also A.A. Hodge's commentary on this section in his *The Confession of Faith*.

8. *To all those for whom Christ hath purchased redemption, he doth certainly and effectually apply and communicate the same*; (John 6:37, 39, John 10:15–16) making intercession for them, (1 John 2:1–2, Rom. 8:34) and revealing unto them, in and by the word, the mysteries of salvation; (John 15:13, 15, Eph. 1:7–10, John 17:6) effectively persuading them by his Spirit to believe and obey, and governing their hearts by his word and Spirit; (John 14:16, Heb. 12:2, 2 Cor. 4:13, Rom. 8:9, 14, Rom. 15:18–19, John 17:17) overcoming all their enemies by his almighty power and wisdom, in such manner, and ways, as are most consonant to his wonderful and unsearchable dispensation. (Ps. 110:1, 1 Cor. 15:25–26, Mal. 4:2–3, Col. 2:15).[54]

Here Hodge also cites the Confession of Dort, Ch. ii:1, 2, 8. These statements with their Scriptural applications reveal the false claims the Hulsean party makes for orthodoxy.

Confusing premises with deductions

In 1983 Curt Daniel handed in a doctoral thesis to the University of Edinburgh entitled *Hyper-Calvinism and John Gill*. For 766 pages he condemns a yet undefined Hyper-Calvinism, draws a verbal caricature of John Gill and pleads for a gospel according to duties. Confessing his indebtedness to Andrew Fuller, he concludes:

---

[54] Boyce's *Abstract*, p. 339.

> Hyper-Calvinism is that School of Supralapsarian 'Five Point' Calvinism which so stresses the sovereignty of God by over-emphasising the secret over the revealed will and eternity over time, that it minimizes the responsibility of Man, notably with respect to the denial of the word 'offer' in relation to the preaching of the gospel of a finished and limited atonement, thus undermining the universal duty of sinners to believe savingly with the assurance that the Lord Jesus Christ died for them, with the result that presumption is overly warned off, introspection is overly encouraged, and a view of sanctification akin to doctrinal Antinomianism is often approached.

Normally such a theory is presented at the beginning of an academic thesis to introduce new, independent thought. Supporting arguments are then given leading to a logically grounded conclusion. Instead, Daniel presents a borrowed hypothesis; provides no evidence for it and places his premise where his conclusion should be. He then opens a new theoretical discussion in an appendix concerning whether Calvin was a particularist or a universalist, suggesting that Calvin was at times the one and at times the other according to which of the two wills of God he was talking about. Daniel thus jumps from an unproven hypothesis to pure speculation concerning the mind of Calvin and the imagined inconsistency of God. None of this is academically, historically or theologically convincing.

Gill was no Supralapsarian

Daniel claims that all Hyper-Calvinists are Supralapsarians (p.749), therefore Gill is a Supralapsarian, though Daniel never clearly defines the term so we are left somewhat in the dark as to his meaning. Yet, Gill was demonstrably not a Supralapsarian as he explained at length himself.[55] John Rippon and Augustus Toplady vouched for this truth. Indeed, Rippon spends four pages of his brief biography of Gill, weighing up his subject's attitude to the Lapsarian controversy, coming down for Gill on the Sublapsarian side and arguing with Gill that it was a mere academic point over which it was quite unnecessary to fall out.[56] In rejecting such primary and secondary sources, Daniel severely weakens his theory. Daniel also lists Gill's friend Toplady as a Supralapsarian, though Toplady shows clearly in his *Historic Proof of the Doctrinal Calvinism of the Church of England* that Sublapsarianism was his own doctrine and that of the English Reformers. He also criticized Supralapsarianism strongly. If Daniel had been my student, I would have told him that I did not want a compendium of quotes but original, reasoned, Biblical and historical arguments leading to his own grounded conclusions.

---

55 See, for instance, Gill's *Truth Defended* (1736), against Job Burt's charges of Supralapsarianism.

56 *Life of John Gill*, pp. 48-51. The essence of the distinction is as follows: *Supralapsarian*: God decreed to elect certain individuals prior to and independent of the fall. *Sublapsarian*: God elected certain individuals from the fallen masses. This distinction, as Gill points out, is merely academic. Objections to both sides are even more speculative. Supralapsarianism, it is argued, makes God the author of sin. Sublapsarianism robs God of His immutability. The discussion rarely proves helpful and the terms have caused much theological confusion. Common grace preachers use the term Supralapsarian to denounce their orthodox opponents, although the cap rarely fits. Actually, common grace preachers are nearer Supralapsarianism as they do not take the fall seriously in God's electing and reprobating purposes.

Gill knew only God's revealed will

Daniel nowhere proves that God has two wills, whether secret or revealed, volitional or decretal. Gill taught that all we know about God savingly is through revelation and Daniel provides no evidence that his supposed Hypers professed to proclaim God's unrevealed secrets. What Daniel thinks is taboo in preaching our Reformers thought was the most comforting part of the gospel. Daniel affirms that his Hypers are in error regarding God's sovereignty but he does not define God's sovereignty so that we might follow his argument. Here Daniel sides with those common-gracers who believe that the teaching of the church throughout all ages has been that God is in conflict with Himself and with His Son because of His wavering between two wills. This is an erroneous view. The so-called Church Fathers, like the Reformers, are mostly unanimous in declaring that the common-grace gospeller's view of God divided against Himself is heretical. For instance, under the heading: *The will of the omnipotent God is never defeated,* in his doctrinal work *Enchridion*, chap. CIII, Augustine says:

> But however strong may be the purpose either of angels or of men, whether of good or bad, whether these purposes fall in with the will of God or run counter to it, the will of the Omnipotent is never defeated; and His will can never be evil; because even when it inflicts evil it is just, and what is just is certainly not evil. The omnipotent God, then, whether in mercy He pitieth whom He will, or in judgment hardeneth whom He will, is never unjust in

> what He does, never does anything except of His own free-will, and never wills anything that He does not perform.

Augustine believed in addressing all with the full gospel but not the watered-down, common grace, duty faith novelty. He also believed, like Gill, that God's plan of salvation addresses the fallen masses, which is the Sublapsarian view.

Chosen to salvation from eternity

In arguing that Hypers emphasise the eternal rather than the time-bound, Daniel appears to belittle the fact that preaching the Gospel is to prepare people for eternity, a calling which is given from eternity, based on a salvation activated from eternity. What is the point of salvation if it is not eternal? The idea of salvation from eternity possibly upsets Daniel because it totally rules out man's agency. Where the Scriptures teach that 'salvation is of the Lord', there is not even a marginal reference which says, 'Some MSS add "Taking man's agency into consideration."' Such later glosses are unknown! Speaking of those who wrongly argue for human agency in salvation and declare 'It is not of God that showeth mercy, but of man that willeth,' Augustine says:

> The true interpretation of the saying, 'It is not of him that willeth, nor of him that runneth, but of God that showeth mercy,' is that the whole work belongs to God, who both makes the will of man righteous, and thus prepares it for assistance, and assists it when it is prepared. (*Enchridion,* Chap. XXXII)

Incidentally, these Church Fathers preached that man is like a dead dog spiritually unless the Holy Spirit makes him *sensible* to his state. This is Hyper-Calvinism to Daniel, Hulse and the Murrays, yet it was also the glorious preaching of the 18th century Awakening.

Man responsible for his sin but not for his salvation

Daniel's insistence that Gill minimized human responsibility in salvation takes us to the heart of common-grace gospel thinking. Expounding John 5:40, Gill says clearly:

> ... his not coming to Christ, when revealed in the external ministry of the gospel, as God's way of salvation, is criminal and blame-worthy; since the disability and perverseness of his will are not owing to any decree of God, but to the corruption and vitiosity of his nature, through sin; and therefore, since this vitiosity of nature is blameworthy; for God made man upright, though they have sought out many inventions, which have corrupted their nature; that which follows upon it, and is the effect of it, must be so too.

This both absolves Gill from any suspicion of Supralapsarianism and of any suspicion that he might believe that natural man is not responsible for his rejection of Christ. But this is not enough for Daniel. He claims that Gill minimizes human responsibility 'notably with respect to the denial of the word "offer" in relation to the preaching of the gospel of a finished and limited atonement, thus undermining the universal duty of sinners to believe savingly with the assurance that the Lord Jesus Christ died for them.'

Daniel has jumped to false conclusions again. Gill does not challenge the use of the word 'offer' at all with reference to a finished and particular atonement. The only time he speaks against using the word 'offer' is in relation to a universal atonement, universally offered to each and every man with a warranty that they have a right to it. Otherwise, Gill makes it clear that he has nothing against such words as invitations and exhortations. Nor would Gill be so theologically confused as Daniel to offer a finished and limited atonement with the warrant or assurance that it is unfinished and universal. Here, Daniel is taking human responsibility too far as a result of his low view of God's sovereignty and high view of man's ability. Though man is responsible for his fall, he is irresponsible in matters of salvation and thus doubly blameworthy. Without God's agency, man cannot recognize this, nor can he recognize the irresponsibility of his behaviour in rejecting Christ. It is irresponsible of Daniel to suggest otherwise.

Part 4: The Gospel Of Saving Grace

A leap in the dark

Common-grace gospellers love to speak about joining opposites by accepting paradoxes. They see contradictions in the will of the Father, disagreements within the Trinity and inconsistencies in the Word of God. Only by believing both sides of a paradox, they argue, can one come to a saving knowledge of the Truth. This sounds like the way-off dogma of existentialist philosopher Kierkegaard who believed one could find saving illumination by leaping into the dark. Yet, where Scripture clearly states that there is a marked difference between the knowledge of God gained in nature and that gained through Christ's redemptive acts, the common-gracers claim this is a false distinction. Thus they see diversity where there is unity and unity where there is diversity.

Scripture divided against itself

This low view of the gospel, grace and the Godhead and high view of man expressed in common-grace teaching is built on a radically wrong view of Scripture. The Word of God is like a two-sided banner, they tell us. One side depicts one insignia, the other side another, but it is all one banner. This two sided view of the Banner of Truth is displayed in Issue 371-372, p. 42 ff. of their magazine and the *Evangelical Times* (August 1996, p. 19) where David Gay outlines his theory of a self-contradictory God revealing Himself in a self-contradictory Bible. They preach that we must accept the contradictory nature of the Scriptures as this reflects God's two minds, but common grace, properly utilized by man provides the bridge over this great divide. This is the old Liberal heresy that natural law is superior to revealed law. In a most unpastoral pastoral letter for 1807 entitled *Moral and Positive Obedience*, Fuller claims:

> The obligation of man to love and obey his Creator was coeval with his existence; but it was not till God had planted a garden in Eden, and there put the man whom he had formed, and expressly prohibited the fruit of one of the trees on pain of death, that he came under positive law. The former would approve itself to the conscience as according to the nature of things; the latter as being commanded by his Creator.

Inherent moral obligation superior to revealed command

Fuller argues further that natural obligations are superior to God's revealed positive will as natural obligations are right in themselves but God might have commanded the opposite if He had so willed. At the root of all Fuller's exegesis is his effort to isolate passages dealing with 'the nature and fitness of things', i.e. natural law, from God's own expressions of His decretal will. In his pastoral letter, Fuller strives to define what is right because it is right in itself and what is right merely because God commands it.

Confusing the common with the special

Common-grace gospellers are open to severe criticism in their appeal to natural theology in order to lift up man savingly. Though they speak so much of climatic and geological conditions as the basis of their gospel, they give this a Scriptural varnish by claiming that highly soteriological texts dealing with God's treatment of His loved-ones must be drawn down into this category and are thus valid for all. Two of their favourite texts to this end are Isaiah 55:1ff.[57] and 1 Timothy 2:3, 4. Here, they claim Andrew Fuller and John Calvin as their mentors.

We must agree concerning Fuller, but Calvin cannot be quoted as their mentor. He uses the Suffering Servant passages to demonstrate that God's mercy is not universal, yet Hulse calls Isaiah 55 (Ho, every one that thirsteth, come ye to the waters), a 'Text of Reasoning' against those who 'deny that faith is a duty' and sees in it a demonstration of common grace, revealed to all.[58] Fuller tells us, 'The thirst which they are supposed to possess does not mean a holy desire after spiritual blessings, but the natural desire of happiness which God has planted in every bosom.' He concludes, 'The whole passage is exceedingly explicit, as to the duty of the unconverted; neither is it possible to evade the force of it by any

[57] This text has been given more attention in my *The Free Offer and the Call of the Gospel*.

[58] *The Free Offer*, pp. 14, 24.

just or fair method of interpretation.'[59] Both Hulse and Fuller call this 'a gospel offer', answering the needs of human duties and natural desires for happiness. This is a far cry from eternal salvation which answers the love of God for His people.

A gospel which claims that it is the duty of all men to cater for natural reason and happiness can never produce that holiness without which no man shall see the Lord. This becomes more evident when one realises that Fullerism rejects the doctrine of Christ's imputed righteousness which is so essential to the doctrine of saving grace and equally essential for the believer's sanctification. This was held by all those men of God who common-gracers scorn. Hulse and Fuller fail to explain how satisfaction of natural desires can lead to a holy, righteous life. Yet Hulse concludes from the above that 'There is no contradiction between particular redemption and the free offers of the Gospel to all men, ... This offer is neither vain nor fruitless, being declarative of their duty.' Anything else, Hulse argues, 'minimise(s) the moral and spiritual responsibility of sinners.' On the contrary, Hulse maximises man's fallen capacities and so minimises Christ's saving work.

In context, however, we see that Isaiah's words refer to those hungering and thirsting for God's *righteousness* and not for 'a *natural desire* of happiness'. The previous chapter tells these thirsty ones that their Maker and Redeemer is their husband, pledged in mercy to them for ever. The verse before 55:1 proclaims 'This is the heritage of the servants of the Lord, and their righteousness is of me, saith the Lord'. Righteousness is a family matter.

---

[59] *Works*, Vol. II, p. 344.

Murray's misuse of Spurgeon

Attempting to present an Arminian Spurgeon in his *Spurgeon v. Hyper-Calvinism*, Iain Murray makes much of what he calls 'the crucial text', quoting from Spurgeon's sermon on 1 Timothy 2:1-4 (Who will have all men to be saved).[60] Here, Spurgeon frankly confesses that he believes God's word as it stands but does not fully understand the text. He then explains what it cannot possibly mean, i.e. that God wills the salvation of all as a result of His divine purpose. Much of Murray's quote is concerned with stories Spurgeon told to illustrate the idea that fools step in where angels fear to tread. Murray has stepped in and does not realize that he is advocating what Spurgeon explicitly refutes.

Whatever Spurgeon's opinions on this matter, which seldom agree with Murray's versions of them, Murray has a hard time arguing that a warrant of salvation can be given to every man on the basis of 1 Timothy 2:3. In context, Paul is speaking of the giving of thanks for 'all men'. He obviously does not recommend thanking God for every man everywhere because he lists special people for whom we are to thank God. Thus elsewhere in the AV, the term translated 'all' is rendered 'all manner' or even 'whomsoever' or 'whatsoever'. Paul tells us that God will have such special dignitaries saved. Now Murray might find here evidence to prove that God desires the salvation of all kings and politicians. We would like this, of course. But this would be straining the text and as Augustine says, 'It is perverse to measure divine will by the standards of human justice.' Incidentally, Augustine expounds 1 Timothy

[60] Pp. 155-157.

2:3, 4 exactly as Paul explains the situation, concluding that God grants to the prayers of the humble the salvation of the exalted and that God never wills to do anything that He does not do.[61]

Murray's fourfold appeal forced on Spurgeon

Murray lists what he calls *Spurgeon's Fourfold Appeal to Scripture* to establish a case for a general call to salvation. We must note, however, that the first 'appeal', headed *God's invitations are Universal*, is voiced in Murray's words, not Spurgeon's. Murray cites the famous 'whosoever texts', Romans 10:13 and Revelation 22:17 and the fact that 'he who believeth on Him is not condemned' (John 3:18). Then Murray allows Spurgeon to say that the same gospel should be delivered to the dead as to the living. The point of distinction is not in the gospel, but in its being applied by the Holy Ghost, or left to be rejected of man.

This is sound enough, but Murray is arguing that misguided Hypers such as Gill and Huntington will not preach to all men, everywhere as the Spirit leads. The truth is that they filled these texts with the full gospel and delighted in winning souls for Christ. Furthermore, Murray's quotes do not prove that Spurgeon used common-grace as a basis for preaching salvation, nor that he believed that all men universally should be offered Christ savingly as a goal of their duties. Indeed, Spurgeon's own words quoted go contrary to common-grace, duty faith teaching and are entirely in the realms of saving grace.

---

[61] *Enchridion*, Man's Free Will, Vol. IX, pp. 247-249.

Murray's second alleged Spurgeonic appeal is a supposed warrant of salvation, applicable to all which Spurgeon allegedly maintained. Spurgeon, we learn, according to a mere half sentence which Murray quotes, taught that it was not man's willingness that gave him a right to believe but his duty, awakened by God's command. Duty comes before will. So faith comes through performing duties without a will to do them! When we look at the full sermon, we find that Murray has provided an emphasis which Spurgeon nowhere gives. Equally dubious is Murray's attempt to lump together Gill and Huntington with those who criticized Spurgeon and took part in the notorious *Earthen Vessel* debate. Spurgeon did not take part in this debate though Murray's entire argument seems to be built on guessing what Spurgeon would have said if he had done so. Spurgeon presents the words Murray quotes in an entirely different context, *absolutely denying* that every man has a warranty for his salvation. Furthermore, Spurgeon speaks of 'man's condition' in my copy, whereas Murray gives 'man's willingness'. Spurgeon's theme is that nobody can come to God unless God draws him. Man's condition (under common-grace) does not give him a right to believe but God's special call does. He then adds that his sermon is, 'a special call to some of you'. This is quite in keeping both with the teaching of Gill and that of Crisp and Huntington.

Admittedly, Spurgeon has difficulties placing rights, duties and willingness in a set order of salvation, overlapping their meanings, but his message is otherwise clear. The external call of the gospel goes out to all who hear but the special call is the work of election, carried out by the convicting and converting work of the Spirit. The warrant of faith, however, is to the truly penitent. Again, this is exactly as taught by John Gill,[62] and quite the opposite to Murray's message.

Murray's third 'appeal', is to human responsibility. Again, Murray speaks for Spurgeon but when Spurgeon is allowed to speak for himself it is in tones reminiscent of Gill, seeing man as being held accountable for his sin and lack of faith. When Spurgeon speaks of two lines of truth, he is not speaking of a paradox but viewing man's hopelessness on one side and God's saving grace on the other. Murray concludes without grounds from this, neither quoting Spurgeon nor Scripture, but John Duncan, that 'Scripture also presents conversion as the work of man.' Again, Murray has quite misrepresented Spurgeon.

Murray's fourth appeal is to the love of God which he finds evidenced in Spurgeon's sermon on Romans 10:20, 21. Here, Spurgeon explains that he has a two-fold aim, to expound a. the doctrines of sovereign grace and b. man's guilt in rejecting God. In reaching this aim, Spurgeon hardly touches on the text but clearly refutes the Fullerite idea that this passage refers to temporal mercies only and shows that Israel was rejected because she rejected God's love. Gill agrees with Spurgeon, but goes far deeper into the exegesis of the text and is far more optimistic. Gill sets the passage in its true, historical setting as an acceptance of Christ by Gentiles, whereas the Jews, as a people, rejected Him. However, Gill, in speaking of the successful worldwide spread of the gospel, emphasises that we should not take this passage as a condemnation of every Jew, citing Paul himself as a marvellous

---

[62] See Effectual Calling, *Body of Divinity*.

example that God still saves individual Jews after their national rejection of Christ. Here Gill is excellently specific and to the point, whereas Spurgeon is theoretical, abstract and unspecific. Murray, however, is so busy philosophising about God theoretically desiring the salvation of all that he thoroughly misses Gill's practical exposition of the text which displays God in action, working out salvation and judgment. Instead, Murray comes up with secret theories which God is supposed to have, of which Spurgeon obviously was not aware. He was too busy practising his faith rather than speculating on an alternative gospel.

Murray concludes that such as Gill restrict gospel invitations; fail to understand the promises of God as a sufficient warrant for faith; minimise human responsibility and deny that God has any love except for the elect. What has become evident in Murray's day-dreaming is that when his and Spurgeon's exegesis is compared with Gill's verse for verse, then one realizes why honest Spurgeon confessed in a letter written in February 1855 that his 'daily labour was to revive the old doctrines of Gill, Owen, Calvin, Augustine and Christ.' Gill has obviously a greater sense of sin and thus a far higher view of salvation than our modern common-gracers. He is also far more practical and accurate in his application of it.

Sadly this irresponsible reasoning on Murray's part, featuring grave misrepresentations of Spurgeon's doctrine and witness beside that of Gill and others has convinced a number of his fellow Christians that Spurgeon was an Arminian and their respect for Iain Murray's former stand has prevented them from accepting what their mentor says critically and with Spurgeon's sermons before them.

A look back to the faith of our fathers

Whilst doing research into Southern Baptist Declarations of Faith recently, I came across many sound confessions regarding evangelism between 1750 and 1858 based solidly on the doctrines of grace now so despised by common grace preachers. These were written at a time of great church planting and enormous growth and often by young Christians who had established many churches before they were even thought old enough to be ordained. Part of one of these declarations, issued in various churches between 1809 and 1822 reads:

> We believe in one only true and living God, who is infinite and unchangeable in all his divine perfections or attributes, such as wisdom, power, justice, love, &c., the Creator and Preserver of all things; and that he cannot be brought under the least obligations to any of his creatures.
>
> We believe that as there is nothing new with God, it is his eternal purpose to save those who ultimately will be received into heaven, not upon the supposition of any condition to be performed by them, but wholly in consequence of what Jesus Christ has done in their behalf.
>
> We believe ... that Christ's life, death, resurrection, and intercession, were, and are, in behalf of those, and those only, who shall enjoy the benefits thereof.
>
> We believe it to be perfectly congenial to the Scriptures, and to the spirit of the foregoing articles, for

ministers of the Gospel to command all men indiscriminately to repent, and to exhort them to believe the Gospel.

Such declarations, echoed by J. P. Boyce and J. L. Dagg and anchored in the 1858 Southern Baptist Theological Seminary Standards, are in full concord with ancient European protestant Reformed declarations of faith whether Anglican, Presbyterian, Congregational or Particular Baptist. They are particularly one in their witness with the Canons of Dort and the Westminster Confession to which most of these modern common grace evangelists profess allegiance.

On examining these older grounds for Christian witness, we find their basis for evangelism is the atonement and the Great Commission which commands Christians to evangelise all nations. These earlier believers saw themselves as fishers of men, casting out their nets wherever they were sent and drawing in those whom Christ had prepared for eternal life. This picture horrifies evangelists of our modern Reformed Establishment who tell us that evangelization is not based on gathering in those sheep for whom Christ died, who are known by God alone. This, they find, is discriminating and politically incorrect preaching.

God's grace is never common

We find the concept of God's grace used throughout both the Old Testament and the New. In the Old Testament Messianic Psalm 45:2, the King is addressed with the words 'Thou art fairer than the children of men: grace is poured into thy lips: therefore God hath blessed thee for ever.' Psalm 84:11 tells us, 'For the Lord

God is a sun and shield; the Lord will give grace and glory: no good thing will he withhold from them that walk uprightly.' A further Messianic verse in Zechariah 12:10 refers to God's pouring the spirit of grace and supplication upon the House of David. These Old Testament passages use the words חֵן (chên) and חָנַן (chânan) which have the root meanings 'favour' and 'loving-kindness'. The words are invariably used to express God's Divine love given freely to whomsoever He will. There is no reference to such a grace given generally to either nature or man.

In the New Testament, the Greek word *charis* is used in the same sense as its OT counterparts, with the emphasis being on the undeserved favour of God. Thus, in 1 Corinthians 15:10 Paul can testify, 'But by the grace of God I am what I am: and his grace which was bestowed upon me was not in vain; but I laboured more abundantly than they all: yet not I, but the grace of God which was with me.' The Apostle further testifies in Ephesians 3:7, 'Whereof I was made a minister, according to the gift of the grace of God given unto me by the effectual working of his power.'

This grace is seen as a saving, effectual attribute mediated by the Lord Jesus Christ and is thus often referred to in the New Testament as 'the grace of our Lord Jesus Christ.' Thus in Acts 15:11 Peter says, 'But we believe that through the grace of the Lord Jesus Christ we shall be saved.'[63] As in the Old Testament, grace in the New is always initiated by God as an act of His will and is never general but always specific.

---

[63] See also Romans 16:20; Revelation 22:21 etc..

Grace is always something special

The grace of the Lord Jesus Christ is always described as being solely for God's elect and the very opposite of general, human endeavour. Thus Paul can say in Romans 11:5-7:

> Even so then at this present time also there is a remnant according to the election of grace. And if by grace, then is it no more of works: otherwise grace is no more grace. But if it be of works, then is it no more grace: otherwise work is no more work. What then? Israel hath not obtained that which he seeketh for: but the election hath obtained it, and the rest were blinded.

In Ephesians 1:7 Paul tells us that we have redemption through Christ's blood and the forgiveness of sins according to the riches of His grace. In Galatians 5:4 he tells us that Christ is of no effect for those who wish to be justified by the law. Such is, indeed, a sure sign that one is bereft of or 'fallen from grace'. Indeed, the New Testament has not a word to say concerning a common grace that leads us to God but everything to say about a saving grace which draws us to God.

Grace is not inherent in nature

This Biblical truth was challenged by Pelagius, alias Morgan (c.383-c.409), a Welsh enthusiast and humanist moralist who claimed that grace was an integral part of nature and was always there to guide the intellect to God. Whereas Augustine emphasized that nature fell with man and thus has nothing to tell him about saving grace, Pelagius postulated that nothing sinful held man's will in bondage but man has the natural capacity to choose the way he wished to go. Thus man, like his progenitor Adam, is a probationer and grace is the probation officer or external natural help which points man to the right use of his capabilities. This is the ground of modern forensic psychiatry which teaches 'Criminal – heal thyself', and our Selfist leftovers from Kantianism and that dark period in history called the Enlightenment which boasts categorically, 'I can, I must and therefore I will'. Indeed, this is how Arthur Kirkby in his excellent doctoral thesis sums up Fuller's soteriological theology, in the words 'He could if he would'.[64] Pelagius' theory lies at the heart of common grace, duty faith teaching. Our Reformers, therefore, in order to rescue us from Pelagian Rome, stressed that not only our wills were in bondage to sin by nature but all our human capacities. However, true, saving grace points to the death of all natural religion and the self-determination of man, leaving him with no natural abilities with which to reach out and grasp God. Yet, in the enthusiasm of preaching, the temptation to stoop too low and talk down to the self-pride of our hearers is great and sadly the best of us fall into this temptation. This is the only explanation I have for the fact that a most renowned evangelist and pastor of strong Puritan persuasion, whilst commenting favourably on Iain Murray's unbalanced comparison of Spurgeon with alleged Hyper-Calvinism, outdid Murray and pronounced that salvation was 'God doing all and man also doing all'.[65] This is Pelagianism pure.

---

[64] *The Theology of Andrew Fuller in its Relationship to Calvinism*, Edin., 1956, p. 160.

[65] Geoffrey Thomas, Evangelical Times, July 1995, p. 11.

No human responsibility without God's sovereignty

The true grace which saves is all of God and, as the early church taught, it comes a. *preveniently*, stopping men in their tracts, like Paul on the way to Damascus, and lifting them out of sin, pointing them to the Saviour; b. *co-operantly*, moving them to seek righteousness and work righteously; and c. *irresistibly*, for God is all-sovereign in matters of salvation. God's sovereignty can never be over-emphasized above man's responsibility as the common-gracers teach. On the contrary; it is God's absolute sovereignty alone that *defines* wherein man's responsibility lies and, as a consequence, *dooms* man for being responsible for his sins. When common-gracers deny this absolute sovereignty, they deny man's responsibility for his sin. Consequently, those who say that salvation is all of God and all of man are ridiculing God's sovereignty and making a god of man. It is God's sovereignty alone that can forgive man's irresponsibility and irresponsiveness in not following Him. How can one over-emphasise this saving truth?

So much for common grace, or rather its non-existence in God's plan of salvation. But such as Hulse, Watts, Johnson, the Murrays and the Banner of Truth team tell us that it is here in this non-entity that the gospel begins. We must therefore look at the Biblical doctrine of the gospel.

The nature and scope of the gospel

The Lord Jesus Christ opened His ministry in Nazareth by declaring that the Spirit of the Lord was upon Him and that He had been appointed to preach the gospel. So immediately, we see that as Christ is the direct source of grace, so He is also the direct source of the gospel. Both grace and the gospel emanate from our Redeemer.

Here, Christ is referring back to the Old Testament prophesy in Isaiah 61 where the prophet speaks of Christ being anointed by the Spirit to preach glad tidings. In the Greek Septuagint the word used for 'glad tidings' is the same as the New Testament term for 'gospel' but the word used in the Hebrew Old Testament (*bahsar*) is of great exegetical significance. It is the same root as used in words to do with 'flesh' or 'incarnation'. Our English word 'bazaar' which originally meant a meat market, testifies to this usage. A good tiding was one which was not only theoretical but one which 'became flesh', i.e. it was fulfilled before the eyes and ears of the recipients. Isaiah, of course, is the great spokesman of the Incarnation, preaching 'Unto us a child is born, unto us a son is given'. Thus the birth of the Lord Jesus was proclaimed to the shepherds as 'good tidings of great joy' and John tells us that 'the Word became flesh'. The gospel took on form, not in nature but in the Person of the Lord Jesus Christ.

The gospel per definition points to Christ's saving work

The fact that, like grace, the gospel per definition is bound up with the Person of Christ is clear from the NT references which introduce the gospel as the *Gospel of the Lord Jesus Christ the Son of God* (Mark 12:1) and the *Glorious Gospel of Christ* (2 Corinthians 4:4) and thus the *Gospel of Grace* (Acts 20:24). As this gospel is bound up with the saving work of Christ's grace, it is the *Gospel of Salvation* (Ephesians 1:13 etc.). It is also called the *Gospel of Peace* (Ephesians 6:15 etc.) because it is the only gospel that can reconcile a sinner to

God. Through this reconciliation, the saved sinner is given entrance into the Kingdom of God and thus we are told that this is the *Gospel of the Kingdom* (Matthew 4:23).

... And to the preaching of this work

Isaiah is also our link in the pan-Biblical calling to preach the gospel. The prophet proclaimed in chapter 52:7:

> How beautiful upon the mountains are the feet of him that bringeth good tidings that publish peace; that bringeth good tidings of good, that publisheth salvation; that saith unto Zion, Thy God reigneth.

Here we have the NT teaching on the height, depth and breadth of the gospel in a nutshell. Paul thus makes this verse one of the pillars of his calling to show the discriminating work of the gospel in the hearts of both Jews and Gentiles (Romans 10:15-21), choosing out those who did not seek God of themselves and rejecting those who made an empty profession of being under the gospel. If this gospel is hid, it is hid to those who are lost (2 Corinthians 4:3).

The ground of salvation is solely saving grace

There is thus no general gospel that shines into all hearts and no gospel of common grace that leads sinful man from the natural via deduction to the supernatural. The ground of our salvation is through the gospel of saving grace alone and this is all of God and none of man. The way to approach God is not through nature, not through common grace, not through the moral law, not through duty-faith and not through universal offers. It is only through tearfully and repentantly pleading for the saving grace of Jesus that sinners are saved, drawn by the cords of God's love. There is only one way into Heaven, and that is when Christ opens the door. 'By grace are ye saved through faith; and that not of yourselves: it is the gift of God' (Ephesians 2:8).

Christ, touched by our infirmities

Those evangelists of old, now scorned for their high view of God's sovereignty in salvation, did not fail to tell sinners that Christ was touched with the feelings of their infirmities. Indeed, they taught that only when a sinner experiences that he is infirm through and through in his very nature and being can he begin to realize under the working of the Spirit how very lost he is. Robert Hawker is one of those ridiculed by our modern common grace scoffers as a Hyper-Calvinist of sterile, severe and dry religion. Yet he filled churches to bursting point wherever he preached because he never lost sight of the lowliness of man and his needs and the high glory of God who dispenses His balm of Gilead. Speaking to his simple cottagers who were becoming well-trained theologians through years of Hawker's marvellous ministry, the faithful pastor could assure them from the Scriptures (Hebrews 4:15):

> If I have been happy enough to establish by this scriptural statement, the blessed truth itself, and shewn you, by infallible testimony, that Jesus is 'touched with the feelings of our infirmities,' and that these gracious and endearing feelings of our Lord are the result of the ancient engagements of all the persons in the Godhead,

nothing will remain to finish our subject but the accompaniment of the Holy Ghost in his divine teachings, to lead out our hearts, and the hearts of all that hear these things, to know what personal knowledge you have, that such tender manifestations of Christ have been, and now are, in your experience: this is the important result, as it concerns us in our individual circumstances. In whatever point of view the subject be considered, the consciousness of this tender sympathy of our Lord to the feeling our infirmities meets every case, and suits all the situations however diversified of his people. It is impossible that any sinner can be so desperately driven by the enemy of souls, or the corruption of his own nature, (where the Lord hath given a sense to feel sin,) but may find comfort that Christ is 'touched by the feeling of his infirmities.' None so hopeless, none so helpless, as to preclude either Christ's commiseration, or Christ's power to deliver.[66]

Here, too, we must again think of Crisp who never stopped preaching *Christ the Only Way*, though he risked his life at times doing so. Many were the evil ministers who told downright lies to 'prove' that saintly Crisp was an Antinomian. Speaking on John 14:6 the great evangelist proclaims:

In the first place, There is this great and ineffable excellency and accommodation in Christ, the way, that

[66] From *Jesus touched with the Feeling of Our Infirmities*, preached at Charles, Plymouth 10 April, 1825. Taken from *Village Sermons*, Vol. 1.

he is a free way for all comers to enter into, without any cause of fear, that they shall trespass by entering: he is a free way, I say: a way that costs nothing; a way barred up to no person whatsoever; a way whose gates are cast off from the hinges; nay, rather, a way that hath no gates at all into it; a cheap way to us, a costly way indeed unto the Father, and to Christ, too ... Christ is a free way for the vilest sort of sinners, as for any person under heaven. If Christ hath given a heart to a sinner, to set footing into himself; that is, to receive, to take him for his Christ; if Christ hath given him a heart to take him for his Christ in reality, to take him truly and unfeignedly: Christ is a way for such a person to the Father, though he be the vilest person under heaven. And he is to him a way unto the Father, even while he is ungodly, before he is amended; and he may take his part in this Christ as an ungodly person, as well as when he is righteous. In this regard, I say, Christ is a free way; God looks for nothing in the world from the sons of men, be they what kind of men soever, he looks for nothing from them, to have a right to Christ; but he did freely give Christ unto them, without considering of any thing that they might bring along with them.[67]

Setting an Anti-Christ on Christ's throne

Richard Alderson, in his *No Holiness, No Heaven!*, castigates William Romaine in an appendix borrowed from John Angell

---

[67] *The Sermons of Tobias Crisp*, Issue 1, pp. 38, 39.

James, for being too Christo-centric, (i.e. He preached that salvation was all of Christ), and complains that this kind of preaching leads to 'theoretic Antinomianism' as it only deals with the centre and not the circumference. We read, 'Christ is the centre of the Christian scheme, but there is also a circumference; and a true faith, while it begins at the centre, does not stop there, but radiates through all the intermediate spaces to the outer circle.'

We are told further that Romaine's gospel 'must be considered by every judicious mind as defective,' though the writer's own gospel is apparently very near to Gnosticism and he forgets that Paul says, 'I preach Christ and Him crucified', with not a word about circles, radiations and circumferences. Christ was all to Paul and Christ was all to Romaine. As the old hymn says, 'None but Christ can satisfy.' Christ as a mere centre but not that which radiates from it, is a strange gospel indeed. One is reminded here of what James Ussher told James I on 18 February, 1620:

> Out of Christ there is nothing but confusion; without Him we are nothing but disordered heaps of rubbish, but in Him all the building fitly framed together, growth unto an holy temple in the Lord. Of ourselves we are but lost sheep, scattered and wandering in every direction. From Him it is that there is one fold and one Shepherd.

In that holy temple, Christ, our Great High Priest, King of Kings and the Shepherd of our souls ministers to us alone. He has no human agent doing the work of grace for Him, though He uses His saints to proclaim that grace. Thus, the only agency of man which exists in gospel work is that of Christ's ambassadors after their conversion. Before salvation man's agency is neither required nor possible. Therefore, those who say that salvation is all God's work and all man's work place a rival god on Christ's throne and thus invent for themselves an Anti-Christ.

The proper place of law and grace

Few preachers stressed law and grace in their proper places as Romaine who saw Christ working through both, yet both were not identical to Him. Hear Romaine preaching passionately to lost sinners on law and grace from Romans 3:27, 'Where is boasting then? It is excluded. By what law? Of works? Nay, but by the law of faith.'

> The righteousness which is the ground and matter of our justification, is called in scripture, 'the righteousness of faith,' because faith receives it and applied it, and 'the law of faith' because the sinner is obliged to accept of this by faith only; and the manner of his receiving it is by imputation. As Christ took our sins upon him, and was a sinner by imputation, he was made sin for us, who knew no sin; so we are made the righteousness of God IN HIM; not righteous in ourselves inherently, but in him: we are righteous only in him: his righteousness is imputed to us, and made ours by faith, even as Abraham believed God, and it was imputed to him for righteousness. And in this way of justifying a sinner through imputed righteousness the moral law is so far from being made void, that it is established, and the great end of it is answered; for the

apostle says, 'Christ is the end of the law for righteousness to every one that believeth.' The end of the law was to justify those who keep it; 'Do this, and thou shalt live;' but we attain not to this end, because, through the corruption of our nature, we do not keep the law perfectly; but Christ fulfilled the law for all those who believe in him, and therefore he became the end of the law for righteousness to every one that believeth. By believing we receive the righteousness, and then we answer the end of the law. Thus the law of faith does infinite honour to the moral law, and the believer is continually glorifying it; for his language is this – I acknowledge the law of God, to be perfectly holy, just, and good; it requireth nothing but what is for the glory of the Lawgiver, and for the good of his creatures; and no satisfaction can be made to its honour and dignity, after it has been once broken, but what is infinitely meritorious, which no sinner can possibly pay. But thanks be to God for the unspeakable gift of Christ's righteousness, which by faith is mine. His active and passive obedience are imputed unto me for righteousness; and I can now give glory to the moral law of God by acknowledging myself to be justly condemned by it, and by placing my whole trust and confidence in Jesus Christ, who of God is made unto me righteousness. Thus the moral law is established. It was fulfilled in Christ, and the end of it is answered in believers; from whence it appears, that the law of faith has provided a full security for the honour and dignity of the moral law, and has magnified it and made it honourable, not only in the way of justifying sinners, but also in their walk and conversation after they are justified; which is the second argument I shall bring in defence of the apostle's doctrine.

The so-called Antinomian goes on to say:

Lord, what love have I unto thy law! I see the holiness, and goodness, and justice of it; yea, I love it above gold and precious stones. Oh! Give me strength that I may keep it with my whole heart. And the Holy Spirit does wonderfully strengthen believers in keeping it ... although Christ has delivered him from the curse of the law, yet with his understanding he assents to its being for God's glory, and for his own interest, to walk in the law of the Lord ... So far then is faith from making void the moral law, that it establishes it as a rule of life for the believer who endeavours by his holy walking to glorify it.

Hervey: preacher of righteousness

Yet these doctrines are called 'Antinomian,' i.e. anti-God's law, by modern Babel of Untruth adherents. So, too, James Hervey, known as the Preacher of Righteousness from the mid-18th to the end of the 19th century and whose books were reprinted with several editions per year for a hundred years, is now ranked with the Antinomians. This is mainly because of Wesley's scandalous tales told about him, the fact that Andrew Fuller disagreed with him but Gill and Toplady, beside Whitefield, loved him. Furthermore, Hervey placed Christ's imputed righteousness high in his doctrinal preaching. Hervey is also criticised by our modern would-be Calvinists because he preached reconciliation on the cross and not at the evangelist's beck and call. This frail invalid not only filled his Anglican country church but the windows had to be taken out so that the crowds who had walked up to twelve miles to hear him could receive the gospel. Listen to him as he preaches on 2 Corinthians 5:18 on the Ministry of Reconciliation:

> Let me now, conformably to my sacred commission, beseech you all to be reconciled. Especially let me beseech the humble penitent, and the haughty self-righteous moralist. Ye humble penitents, that are convinced of sin, and mourn for sin, be of good comfort: God has abounded in the riches of his grace towards you, and has given you a ransom to rely on, of higher dignity than all heavens, of more value than all worlds. The men of Tyre made Blastus, the king's chamberlain, their friend, Acts 12:20; the God of glory has constituted his dear Son your atoning sacrifice, your prevailing advocate. The men of Tyre desired conditions of peace; the Lord Jesus hath obtained and fulfilled the conditions of your peace. Could there be a more glorious person chosen to act as your reconciler, than the Prince of heaven, and heir of all things? Could there be a more effectual method of reconciliation, than his obedience unto death, even the death of the cross? Fly then to this all-sufficient Redeemer. Rely on his most meritorious and satisfactory sufferings. Be your sins ever so numerous, ever so enormous, these need be no bar to your acceptance. For God has received an atonement; an

> infinite atonement God has received. So that he can admit you to his favour, unworthy as you are, without the least blemish to his avenging justice. He can, he will admit you as freely, as if you had never done amiss. Trust, therefore, in your reconciling Saviour. Place a cheerful confidence in his propitiating merits. Only let the grace of God, which has appeared with such transcendent loveliness in the bleeding Jesus, let this grace teach you, with a prevailing efficacy, 'to deny all ungodliness and worldly lusts, and to live soberly, righteously, and godly, in this present world.'

Oh for more of such preaching today! Oh for grace to receive it!

The heart of Hart

And finally, a few verses from a great hymn-writer who, sad to say, is criticised amongst our modern pseudo-intellectual common-grace gospellers for his heart-rendering gospel of the doctrines of grace and allied with those pseudo bogey-men the Antinomians and Hyper-Calvinists. Listen to Joseph Hart expounding Isaiah 55 in its correct Biblical setting, with its correct Biblical message:

> Come, ye sinners, poor and wretched,
> Weak and wounded, sick, and sore;
> Jesus ready stands to save you,
> Full of pity, joined with power;
> He is able,
> He is willing; doubt no more.

Let not conscience make you linger,
Nor of fitness fondly dream;
All the fitness he requireth,
Is to feel your need of him,
This he gives you,
'Tis the Spirit's rising beam.

Come, ye weary, heavy laden,
Lost and ruined by the fall;
If you tarry till you're better,
You will never come at all.
Not the righteous,
Sinners Jesus came to call.

Index Of Bible Verses

www.ingramcontent.com/pod-product-compliance
Lightning Source LLC
Chambersburg PA
CBHW020458100426
42812CB00024B/2697

* 9 7 8 1 9 0 8 4 7 5 0 9 1 *